ASIAN CHRISTIAN SPIRITUALITY

앤 바스토우
톰 드라이버

두 분에게 드립니다.

You will be remembered by
us as inspiring friends
in our common search for
spirituality in this land
of too many spirits —

      December, 1992
on your second visit to
our home in Seoul —

ASIAN CHRISTIAN SPIRITUALITY

Reclaiming Traditions

Edited by

Virginia Fabella
Peter K. H. Lee
David Kwang-sun Suh

ORBIS BOOKS

Maryknoll, New York 10545

Second Printing, September 1992

The Catholic Foreign Mission Society of America (Maryknoll) recruits and trains people for overseas missionary service. Through Orbis Books, Maryknoll aims to foster the international dialogue that is essential to mission. The books published, however, reflect the opinions of their authors and are not meant to represent the official position of the society.

Published by Orbis Books, Maryknoll, NY 10545
Published in Asia by the Ecumenical Association of Third World Theologians, P.O. Box 314, Greenhills 1502, Philippines
Manufactured in the United States of America

Library of Congress Cataloging-in-Publication Data

Asian Christian spirituality : reclaiming traditions / edited by
   Virginia Fabella, Peter K.H. Lee, David Kwang-sun Suh.
        p.   cm.
   Papers presented to the 3rd Asian Theological Conference held in
Korea from July 3 to 8, 1989.
   Includes bibliographical references.
   ISBN 0-88344-800-9
   1. Spirituality—Asia—Congresses.   2. Liberation theology—
Congresses.   3. Sociology, Christian—Asia—Congresses.
4. Christianity and other religions—Congresses.   5. Asia—Religion—
Congresses.   I. Fabella, Virginia.   II. Li, Keng-hsin.   III. Sŏ,
Kwang-sŏn.   IV. Asian Theological Conference (3rd : 1989 : Korea)
BV4485.5.A84   1992
248'.095—dc20   91-38771
                                                                      CIP

Contents

1

Introduction

Virginia Fabella, Peter K. H. Lee,
David Kwang-sun Suh

Asia is traditionally the home of the great religions and spiritualities. It almost seems incongruous and anachronistic that Asians should be in search of an Asian spirituality. But this is precisely what some Asian Christians have begun to do. They have set out in quest of a spirituality that is faithful to their common Christian heritage and at the same time rooted in their own cultures and religious traditions, a spirituality that draws wealth and meaning from the ancient past, yet addresses Asia's contemporary reality as well. This book is the outcome of one such quest.

While today's Asia is rich in natural resources as well as in the antiquity and diversity of its cultures and traditions, most of the continent is poor in basic commodities for its peoples, in opportunities for technical and technological advancement, and in the capacity to be truly interdependent vis-à-vis the industrialized world. In Asia itself, there exist two worlds: the world of the privileged and the world of the marginalized who must struggle for their full humanity or who are too hungry and weakened to struggle at all.

No spirituality that claims to be Asian can disregard the plight of these marginalized and suffering millions, for they are the majority of Asia's people. To be relevant, spirituality in Asia cannot be an elitist or a "pie in the sky" spirituality, but one that responds to people's needs and situations. It must concern

1

itself with people's struggles against dehumanizing economic and political conditions, as well as with their aspirations for a more humane and egalitarian society. It must concern itself with countering those cultural and psychological elements that demean and subjugate, and with creating new patterns of relationships that make life worth living. In a word, spirituality in Asia must be a liberating spirituality.

It is in search of an Asian spirituality of and for liberation that forty Christians, twenty men and twenty women from six Asian countries, gathered at the Ewha Women's University Retreat Center near Suanbo, Korea from July 3 to 8, 1989, to share their stories and experiences and the fruit of their year-long research and communal reflection. We were Catholics and Protestants who came from Hong Kong, India, Sri Lanka, Indonesia, the Philippines, and Korea itself. This gathering was not an isolated event, but was built on two previous meetings that formed part of the Asian program of the Ecumenical Association of Third World Theologians (EATWOT). The first Asian Theological Conference (ATC I), held in Sri Lanka in 1979, focused on the dire conditions in which Asian peoples lived and the attempts of Christians to discover a theology that supported the people's struggle for full humanity. The second conference (ATC II), which took place in Hong Kong in 1984, sought a deeper understanding of the hard reality facing the people of Asia in historical processes. At the same time, it tried to arrive at a common methodology for doing theology in the midst of human struggles. ATC III, as the meeting in Korea was more commonly known, endeavored to expand and deepen the findings of the past ten years with its focus on spirituality.

In articulating a spirituality grounded in praxis, the participants of ATC III hoped to advance Asian people's liberation from all forms of domination. We kept aware of this from the start. Even as we escaped from Seoul's busy traffic to the quiet seclusion of the retreat center nestled among hills and pines, we remained conscious of the tense political climate in our host country: the prevailing issue was the reunification of Korea. University campuses were charged with tear gas as riot police tried to quell demonstrating students; the students were demanding the release of an elderly Protestant minister who had dared to cross the border to meet political leaders and Christians in North Korea. At the same time they were praying for the safe return of Im Soo Kyung, the female university student who defied authorities in order to represent the South Korean student body at the Socialist Youth Festival in Pyongyang. Such events served as reminders that our search for a relevant spirituality cannot be divorced from our peoples' hopes and the ideals for which they struggle and take risks.

Our search together was an engrossing experience. The exchange was intense and honest, stimulated by the opening address given by Samuel Rayan, a Jesuit theologian from India, and spurred on further by the essays from six countries and biblical reflections shared by the participants. These essays, along with a concluding statement that captures both the substance and soul of our week together, comprise the bulk of the present volume.

Rayan's address was inspirational as well as informative and thought provoking. With characteristic depth, Rayan suggests that Asian spirituality can be mined not only from traditional religious sources, but also from people's stories—stories of women, youth, peasants, and other victims of oppression and domination, stories of their struggle for dignity and freedom, of their courage, pain, and hope. Rayan maintains that "the view that Asia is essentially and perennially harmony and peace is a myth," and points to the history of peasant revolts and people's movements against injustice and inhumanity. He examines existing definitions of "spirituality" and shows how they are insufficient and even harmful for their non-historical and otherworldly orientation. In their stead, Rayan proposes an understanding of spirituality in terms of "openness and response-ability" that goes beyond mere accountability to the willingness and readiness to respond to situations of import for life. This spirituality constructs and nurtures what makes for fuller life, for finer humanity, and for a new earth. The Spirit's action in people's lives is thus experienced as an energizing force not only for attitudinal and structural change, but also for "combat" in defense of shared freedom and life in community.

The essays dealing with specific countries formed the major part of the conference. Products of a year-long process of preparation, these essays were written collectively or penned by individuals at their group's commissioning. They were presented in diverse ways, from formal panels to a video presentation by the Philippine delegates. All of these essays revealed that, in varying degrees, "context" and "culture" were determining factors in the search for a liberating spirituality. "Context" dealt mostly with the socioeconomic and political reality, and "culture" with religious roots and tradition.

The Korean report gives emphasis to culture in the search for a liberating spirituality. Acknowledging that Christianity has taken deep roots in the religious soil of Korea, minjung theologians have of late probed more deeply into Korean shamanism as probably the most basic and pervasive form of Korean religiosity or spirituality. Without doubt, Korean shamanism is the religion of the people, the poor, the oppressed and socially marginalized, the minjung. The paper raises the question: Can we find a liberating spirituality in Korean Christianity which has been deeply shamanized? It reexamines shamanism and its *gut* rituals in order to appropriate the liberative elements and energizing life force they generate, and challenges the Korean churches and theological seminaries to incorporate the situation and spiritual tradition of the minjung into their thinking, practice, and educational ventures.

The rest of the reports use a diversity of approaches that reveal the multifacetedness of Asian cultures and realities. The Indonesian paper explores two perspectives in its contribution to an Asian liberation spirituality. One, the perspective of the Javanese world view, centers on the universe as a harmonious unity of the "inner" and "outer" world. The purpose of human life is the well-being of the universe through asceticism and meditation. The second perspective focuses on the concreteness of salvation that involves prayer and praxis, contemplation and action, as inseparable components. Christian spirituality as "the consciousness and means of reaching the vision of God's people" is not contrary to the spirituality of liberation already existing in the people's legends, culture, and practices.

India has a depth of religious traditions that have had a powerful influence on the country's poor who are struggling for life and liberation. While recognizing the wealth of liberative instincts and values enshrined in these traditions, the Indian delegates preferred to highlight three emerging people's movements instead: the *dalit*, the tribal, and the women's movements. *Dalits* are viewed as "outcastes" in the caste hierarchy. They will need a spirituality that "endures conflict and provides hope for the new," since their attempt to regain a new identity and future goes counter to the material interest and the religious hegemony of the ruling caste. The women's movement offers a new paradigm in its critique of patriarchal relationships and modes of decision making. It also expresses a new spirituality in women's solidarity with other oppressed people and in their commitment to heal a wounded world and a wounded creation. The tribal peoples engage in a countercultural movement that envisions an alternative to the existing lifestyle of the nation, and challenges "the 'modern,' scientific, and technological view of life." Their search and struggle as well as their dreams are a manifestation of the deep spirituality of tribal societies. In all these movements, spirituality is an intrinsic element that both inspires and sustains the hope for "a new India and a new world."

Living in a predominantly Christian milieu, the delegates from the Philippines chose to focus on Philippine religiosity. Philippine religiosity takes on many forms, from indigenous religiosity based on animism to folk Catholicism and other popular expressions of Christianity. Previously the values and practices associated with popular religiosity were dismissed as superstition, or seen as obstacles to progress and liberation struggles. However, through case studies it became obvious that in folk religions there are life-giving elements waiting to be tapped. For example, indigenous people have drawn on their own spiritual and religious resources to protect life and land. For them the land is sacred and the whole cosmos is interrelated and interdependent. They strive for wholeness of life. Popular religiosity, then, must be taken seriously, not only by those engaged in struggles for wholeness and liberation, but also by those seeking a spirituality that can support the struggle. A Philippine spirituality of liberation must, therefore, be holistic. It must integrate the liberating aspects of Christian faith and the empowering values and qualities rooted in indigenous religious traditions.

For Sri Lankans, coming from a situation of racial and ethnic conflict and civil strife, context plays a more predominant role. The widespread militarization in the country has had devastating effects on all fronts and areas of life; culture, ethnicity, and religion are often invoked to justify the use of force and violence. In view of the deepening crisis and turmoil, a liberation spirituality for Sri Lanka cannot retreat from conflict and struggle. Christians must face the divisions and antagonisms with the unshaken faith and courage that has produced martyrs in their midst. An escapism from conflict resolution into a dream world of peace is not realistic or authentic. While a liberation spirituality is incarnate in temporal realities, it is based on the ultimate values of the Reign and the fruits of the Spirit: justice, compassion, joy, peace (cf. Matt. 5:3–11; Gal. 5:22–23).

The Hong Kong report, while it also stresses context, presents a different Asian reality. Because this British colony enjoys a certain amount of economic prosperity, people have become captives of the competitive system and commercially-oriented values. Because there is no abject poverty in the colony, they do not think of Hong Kong as Third World, but only in the "shadow of it." Thus it was difficult even for Christians to start talking about a liberation spirituality or to reclaim their Chinese spiritual heritage, for they have been alienated from it. The Chinese students' open demand for liberalization, climaxed in 1989 by the Tiananmen Square massacre, propelled many Hong Kong Christians out of their privatized, complacent spirituality. As they publicly demonstrated their solidarity with the students in China, they reaffirmed their Christian roots and found themselves one with the poor and oppressed. They realized their own need for "liberation from social and economic injustice, from false values and consciousness, from a patronizing form of government." As they face 1997, Hong Kong people have come out of the shadow to live in the light. They can no longer be complacent, but must be prepared for an uphill battle.

The reports sparked comments, questions, and challenges. In small group discussions, the participants asked themselves what liberation spirituality means, what its sources are; how it is rooted in Asian soil; and how it relates to liberation praxis, to sexuality, and to violence. Spirituality is a dynamic quality of life that involves the world and creation, but ultimately comes from a divine source. Thus a spirituality of liberation is a dynamic energy that frees persons, as individuals and as community, to attain a quality of life that endures, and to experience and enjoy the unity and expansiveness of the universe. It is both immanent and transcendent, inward and outward, personal and cosmic.

While a spirituality of liberation was recognized as a grace that bestows power beyond what humans can expect to have of their own accord, it also requires struggle and effort. As one group said, a liberating spirituality is not inward looking; it does not refuse to face hard realities. It demands engagement in movements to emancipate people from enslaving social, economic, and political conditions. This participation "nourishes, sustains, and strengthens our spirituality; our spirituality, in turn, empowers us to participate in liberation struggles." While action is integral to spirituality, so is contemplation. Intellectual understanding or reflection cannot replace prayerful contemplation. Having said this, some participants felt, however, that not enough was said about the contemplative spirituality which is associated with Asian spirituality.

At home with different kinds of spirituality, Asia provides a rich resource for a liberation spirituality. Asia's myths and legends, poetry and drama, its symbols, philosophical writings, and religious texts tell us how people relate to one another and to the ultimate, expanding their minds and spirits. In addition, people's stories of their struggles for life and wholeness inspire and invigorate those who seek a liberation spirituality.

While resources for a liberating spirituality abound, so do obstacles that prevent forward movement: patriarchialism, militarism, capitalism, feudalism, neocolonialism, and consumerism. The institutional church and Western Christian missions did not escape scrutiny or critique. With the naming of these broad and largely "external" obstacles, some felt that in the discussion of this issue we were not self-critical enough. For example, we failed to note our own participation in furthering male domination and other forms of patriarchal practice so pervasive in Asian societies.

Most Asian societies are male oriented and male dominated. Consequently, women have been severely disadvantaged: their education is neglected, their opportunities limited, their role in society restricted. The commercialization of sex has further aggravated women's already subjugated position. In all of this, the female sex is not only the object of economic exploitation, but even the victim of physical abuse and violence.

Sexuality is too often seen as the antithesis of spirituality. As a group we affirmed that human sexuality is part of spirituality and condemned the distorted view and practices which have led to the oppression, victimization, and impoverishment of Asian women. While the social disadvantages women suffer have begun to be overcome, it was acknowledged that in Asia there is still a long way to go before women can be regarded and treated as men's equals. The challenge was posed: What has liberation spirituality to say and to do about sexuality in the Asian setting? What are the churches doing in the face of the distorted understanding of sexuality?

Like sexuality, violence was another topic discussed in relation to spirituality. Violence is not just physical destruction, but also psychological and structural oppression. Traditionally, Asians have been taught to be tolerant. The dominant classes have reinforced their tyranny of the masses by labelling "violent" all those who resist or challenge their oppressive power. Historically the people have risen in armed struggle against the forces of oppression. Recently, "nonviolence" as a stance in resisting evil has been advocated by Christians and "non-Christians" alike. When confronted with concrete situations, however, theoretical understanding or verbal instruction may not be realistic. In such situations, it is up to the people actually involved in the conflict to make the final decision.

Opposing violence is not the same as avoiding suffering. Asians have known suffering as conducive to spiritual growth. But suffering becomes a constructive element in liberation spirituality only if it strengthens the character and spirit of the one who suffers, and at the same time transforms the forces that cause the pain. Suffering may lead to self-sacrifice to the point of death. For Christians, the cross is the paradigm of this principle of self-sacrifice, which calls for great self-discipline and extraordinary courage. But the same principle is known and lived to a greater or lesser extent by adherents of other religions or of no religion at all. In the words of a Beijing student leader who professed no religion, the price of a peaceful protest is sacrifice. Many of the Chinese students gave up their lives that others might *truly* live. This is martyrdom and the ultimate test of a liberation spirituality.

It was clear that, in Asia, liberation spirituality is not the monopoly of Christians. In fact, the majority in liberation movements in Asia are not Christian believers. They include the *dalits*, the tribal, the minjung, both men and women; the growing number of people, many youth among them, in human rights, peace, and ecology movements. Christians form but a minuscule minority in Asia as a whole.

Whatever the source or manifestation of the other liberation spiritualities, if one is to be called Asian *and* Christian, then biblical witness becomes an imperative. One group report states: "One who is involved in a liberation movement can find reinforcement and illuminations from the biblical records." However, like other religious texts, the Bible would have to be read critically. To get the full import of its liberating message, it must be read from the perspective of the poor and oppressed who struggle for the truth, justice, and freedom which the Bible proclaims. It must also be read from an inclusive perspective: Jesus himself respected other points of view, of the stranger, the outcast, the women.

Enriching and stimulating as they were, the group discussions and the essays about particular countries were not the whole of ATC III. Daily Bible studies affirmed that Scripture and our faith tradition were principal sources of our spirituality. Some of these Bible studies are reproduced in this book. There were also prayer and worship together, in small and big groups, that went beyond denominational bounds and reminded us that our search was one. There were visits to a Buddhist shrine and temple, which placed us before one rich source of Asian religious spirituality. And, just as important, there were the exciting experiences of Korean life and culture in the form of a mask dance, of liberation songs, of all kinds of tasty dishes served with *kimchi*, of sleeping dormitory-style on papered floor, of a visit to a Korean home, of a trek through rice paddies to pay respects at an old farmer's shaman shrine.

This book is about spirituality, but it also represents a new way of doing theology. The essays may not be "systematic" as classical theology is wont to be, but they do tell our stories. They are not the product of library research or of one person's brilliance, but the fruit of people's involvement and struggle together. It is a book about a search for an Asian Christian liberation spirituality in our "theo-praxis."

For six days we reflected, worshiped, loved, cried, struggled, laughed, and danced together. We were a community together. On the sixth day, ATC III came to an end, and our hearts were filled with gratitude to all those, far and near, who contributed to our meeting. We issued a final message in free verse form, which to us was more an act of faith than a conference statement. We saw each other's experience of liberating spirituality as a merging flow of river waters into the vast ocean of Asian Christian spirituality. We paused in silence, yes, "before the awesome reality of Asia," but also because of the sacredness of our moments together. We realized that our search together for an Asian liberation spirituality had just begun. We had begun to build "links in a chain that cannot be broken, the chain of experience, welded in love and strengthened by commitment." This we do "through our ability to respond, our openness to reality, our harkening to the Spirit—the ultimate repository of the power that propels us."

Hong Kong, February 3, 1991

2

The Search for an Asian Spirituality
of Liberation

Samuel Rayan

Let us be silent for a moment
Silent before the awesome reality of Asia . . .
Before Asia's vastness, variety, and complexity . . .
Asia's peoples, languages and cultures . . .
Asia's poor, their cries, tears, and wounds . . .
the death of her babies by the millions and
the humiliation of her women . . . and men . . . and their
    struggles.
Let us take Asia to our heart; and
See her and feel her within us.
Embrace her in her wholeness and her brokenness
And let her rivers and her tears flow through us, and
Her winds and her sighs blow within us . . . .

Introduction

In December 1975, the World Council of Churches cele-
brated its Fifth Assembly in Nairobi, Kenya. Many of us assem-
bled in Rome and boarded a plane. We took off and in a few
minutes it was rumored that somebody had a copy of "A Declaration of Conscience," by Kim Chi Ha.[1] That caused the most
excitement of that journey as well as of the succeeding days. Its
witness braced us up. It was a document of committed spiritu-

ality: a document deeply Christian and human, honest and courageous, born of costly liberation struggle, and giving birth to costly liberation struggles.

In Bihar, North India, a *dalit* girl completed high school. (*Dalit* is how the "untouchables" of India call themselves. They make up about one-eighth of the population.) She decided to draw water from a public well, from which the untouchables were kept away by upper castes. She did the forbidden thing and was beaten up. That did not daunt her; she decided to do it again. Now the entire village of untouchables was in danger. Her own people began to discourage her. This hurt her deeply. One day she jumped into the well and ended her life. That last act may be ambiguous, but the protest she voiced is loud and clear, and the word she said to her own people was also loud and clear.

About five years ago, a Christian woman from Kerala, Mary Roy, won a case in the Supreme Court of India. According to a local law passed in 1927 in one of the states of India, Christian women had no right of inheritance. Mary Roy challenged this and won a verdict which struck down the old law as unconstitutional. Roy had to struggle to get a lawyer to argue her case in court. After the judgment, she lost friends and gained enemies. She was looked upon as a cause of unease and bitterness in the Christian communities, though many women were glad.

In the 1920s and early 1930s, Gandhi announced civil disobedience as part of India's struggle for freedom from British colonial control. The campaign included refusal to pay taxes to the British. On the basis of this call, peasants in Western India refused to pay dues to their landlords. The peasants intuited the deeper layers of the structures of oppression. It was not just the British that oppressed. That was but the top layer of domination. The peasants wanted to shake off the yoke laid on them by the landlords, which would otherwise remain even after the British had left. Gandhi failed to appreciate this perception of the peasants.

It is in small and big events like this that we should search for spirituality: people's spirituality and spirituality of and for liberation.

Here is a song, translated from Pilipino.

Come, come and let us listen to the stories
   of what is happening in our times.
Lina was a beautiful girl.
She worked the night shift in a garment
   factory.
She joined the union, participated in a
   mass action.
Suddenly there was a commotion. Lina
   disappeared.
Later when found, she was naked and
   dead.
   Come, come and let us cover her
   nakedness
   And in our hearts let Lina rest.

Pedro Pilapil was a farmer.
He had no other friends but the fields.
But one day strangers came and grabbed
   his fields.
Pedro protested but he was summarily
   killed.
   Come, come and in our hearts
   Let Pedro Pilapil sow his seeds.

Aling Maria and her family
Lived beside a mount of garbage heap.
One day they were bulldozed because
   tourists were coming. Thousands of
   families lost their homes.
   Come, come and in our hearts
   Let Aling Maria build her house.

Come, come and let us resist against
What is happening in our times.[2]

Poverty and oppression, and response to oppression; response of compassion in our hearts; and action of resistance against what is happening.

The stories of the people, what is happening to them, and

what we do with the happenings are the places we mine for spirituality. What Lina did and the risk she took and the price she paid is the spirituality we are talking about. We do—we must do—these things: take into our hearts the victims of oppression together with their courage, pain, and hope; take what is happening today and resist; and let other, more human things happen.

The Nature of Asia

Asia is familiar to us. Its social and cultural geography has often been drawn for us, and so I will not go into an analytical or comprehensive presentation. I shall only try to recall to our memory the reality by speaking a few significant words like caste and class; prejudices and discrimination based on religion, race, ethnic origin, sex; the case of the tribal and indigenous peoples whose lands and forests are being grabbed, ravaged, and flooded, and the people marginalized.

There are two Asias: the Asia of the rich and the Asia of the poor. There are two communities: the privileged elite and the community of the peasantry. This division exists in each region, each country, and between countries too.

> Throughout Asia these two communities in varying degrees have been *in conflict*—with intermittent periods of exhaustion and disengagement—over the long centuries. *Conflict and unrest*, not harmony and order, have been the norm. For the peasants, struggle has been a way of life, not an impulsive departure. Conflict, equated with chaos, prompted *repression* and an imposed discipline.
>
> For the Asian peasant during the several hundred years before the advent of the West, rebellion was a common occurrence. The aftermath of uprisings however was often so devastating, the memory of failure so poignant, that the modern day heirs of the tradition of revolt would not lightly feel moved to raise their battle flags again. Yet for some the haunting memories of past failures had failed; with a hero, a sect, an incident, and rebellion's time had come again.[3]

The view, then, that Asia is essentially and perennially harmony and peace is a myth. In India, we are trying to study the history of peasant revolts. I believe this is being studied in other parts of Asia. That all talk about conflict is anti-Asian is a myth too, a legend fabricated by the elite who would discourage rebellion by painting it un-Asian. *Shanti* and harmony are people's aspirations. They are, as it were, eschatological realities, blessings hoped for and striven after in the processes of struggle against oppression, deprivation and humiliation. The undying pride and self-esteem of the Asian peasants, always rising phoenix-like from the ashes to which repression reduces them, is the measure of their openness to the reality of oppression and to the reality of their own rights. It is also the measure of their "response-ability."

We could also mention:

1) the debt trap into which more and more nations are falling; the aggressive penetration of our countries by multinationals. Most of the time their advent is unnecessary and absurd. Do we indeed need Coca Cola and Pepsi Cola to come to India so we can find something to drink when we are thirsty?

2) the presence of foreign armed forces in Korea, in the Philippines, in the Indian Ocean (the United States has become an Asian military power. This has consequences, not only for our honor, but for our economy, our culture, our politics, and our future); the dumping of nuclear waste in the Pacific and nuclear experiments in the Pacific, whether it be by the United States, or Japan, or France;

3) tourism with its economic and cultural human costs; the unequal distribution of land within each nation and worldwide. The major part of the best land has been occupied by West European white races, and tourism means they are occupying more and more of our land and resources;

4) the worsening ecological situation: pollution through chemical effluent, pesticides, fertilizers, harmful drugs and pseudo medicines, and unnecessary medication. Many of them destroy the health of the soil and the natural healing powers of the human body;

5) education that is still an imitation and echo of the West, through which young people are trained to think with and for

Westerners; development understood in Western terms, irrespective of our history, our resources, our people's needs, and possibilities other than those intuited by the West;

6) women's oppression, which continues from ancient times and only assumes new forms. Within the capitalist business world it has worsened. More and more women and children are becoming commodities through organized prostitution, child labor, and child prostitution;

7) the growing gap between town and rural areas; the imbalance in the use of scarce resources; malnutrition and high infant mortality; the dowry system and India's new invention of bride burning; massive poverty which we mention often.

But there is also people's awakening, with increasing politicization of the masses and growing unrest, which the elite and the oligarchs meet with stepped-up repression. Then there is, on the Asian scene, the socialist experiment with its achievements, its mistakes, its failures, its promises. There is the ecological concern. For instance, several movements exist in my country to protect trees and water and the soil; to prevent multiplication of nuclear plants in the country—that sort of development people do not want. The women's movement is growing stronger and is expanding. It is being realized that, in most countries, the state has ceased to be an agent of social transformation, but instead has become an agent to perpetuate the status quo and the interest of the small ruling elite. Action groups, at variance with governments and with established political parties, are themselves political but choosing a new road.

In conclusion, I would highlight, first, the debt trap, this new imperialism of money. Second, the borrowed development model and the deep dependence that it brings. Third, tourism, which is a new invasion and a subtle form of conquest. Fourth, the presence of the U.S. Army, the United States as an Asian colonizing power. Fifth, scientism, science selling itself to the rich and turning hegemonic and violent, and becoming a destructive force—reductionist science that measures reality, including human reality, in terms of mathematics, quantities and numbers. Sixth, poverty, which means the maldistribution of wealth and resources in each country and across the globe. And seventh, the new spiritual vacuum created by the global economic system of capitalism, a system that was originally atheistic, then donned the mantle of religion for a while, and is now showing its real face again.

On the other side, there are the liberation movements, not only against colonialism of the old type, but against new dominations; and the civil rights movements in every country, the political activists, the resistance to forms of development that are destructive of the masses, but profitable to elite little groups. There is a large number of highly motivated dissenting, politicized voluntary groups. They have considerable experience and understanding of social reality at its grass roots. Political parties and governments have lost contact with the reality on the ground and have become both inept and corrupt. The grassroots organizations are able to relate to diverse sections of the people. And that is where we are looking for new political life.

In addition, there are the trade unions, the peasant movements, the youth organizations, the student body. Can we not add the women's movement? In all this, in all such struggles and movements for dignity and food for the masses, in all such movements, a spirituality is implied. And this spirituality is liberational. It is our task to spell it out and make its resources available for life and for further liberation struggles. If we believe in God as the ultimate and ineluctable imperative of justice, love, freedom, and peace, we must hold that at the basis of every struggle and every move for liberation and life and dignity and rice for the riceless, there is a divine force, there is the Holy Spirit, there is a profound spirituality that, once made explicit, can add clarity, strength, and a sense of direction to life and to struggles for life.

There is something remarkable for an overall Asian scene: it is people inspired by Marx who have been able to resist effectively and successfully the West's armed might. This is true not only of Asia but of Latin America and Africa as well. What does that mean? Is this a theological and a spiritual question?

Asia is people, vast masses of them. Asia is rice and religion. Today Asia is becoming riceless—many people are riceless—and increasingly adopting economic systems and development policies as if people do not matter, as if what mattered is money or statistics or abstractions and scientific immaculateness, which looks for uncontaminated pure soil on which to drop the first atom bomb — Hiroshima and Nagasaki.

The Nature of Spirituality

What then is spirituality? How do we describe it? What are its components? And what is the process of its emergence, development, growth, and maturation?

One kind of spirituality can be described in value-neutral terms. Spirituality is the sum total of one's loves and attitudes; it consists in the ordering of one's loves; it refers to the quality of one's heart and life: quality understood philosophically and not in terms of the fragrance and clarity and beauty that comes from right relationship to God, to people, and to the earth. In this sense, everybody is spiritual or has a spirituality. When I speak of the spirituality of Herr Hitler or of John Rockefeller, the two are kindred spirits; similarly, those who planned and ordered the incineration of Hiroshima. But such a description is of small use.

Another understanding of spirituality rests on religion. Spirituality is often identified with devotions and pious practices, with prayers, sacraments, Bible reading, and so forth. One speaks of spiritual exercises, spiritual reading, spiritual books, and we know what is meant. The spiritual is a particular department of reality opposed to and exclusive of the material, the bodily, the historical, the social, and the political; exclusive especially of the conflictual. This definition seems to concentrate on the salvation of the soul, which is understood as going to heaven. It is interiorizing and other-worldly. It is clearly nonpolitical and distinguishes itself from "mere" social action and "mere" philanthropy.

We consider this way of understanding spirituality insufficient, even harmful, because it rests on a dualistic understanding of reality. It is nonhistorical and other-worldly, and does not concern itself with the transformation of society or the building of the earth. It fails to give sufficient explanation of any kind of incarnation or "descent" of God. It concentrates on interiority and is thus reductionist. It is individualistic and neglects the social which is so essential and vital for the understanding of the human. Thus it is docetist, that is, it holds that this world is unreal, mere insubstantial appearance. And it is elitist. It leaves outside the range of the spiritual the major part of the life of the majority of human beings. It is too monastic, too nonpolitical, abstract, and based on a false anthropology as well as a false reading of the gospel and, I believe, of most scriptures.

For the Christian, spirituality consists of the following of Christ. That would be a third way of describing it. This is a large concept which includes all the modes and modalities of living the life of the kingdom as restored through Jesus Christ. Such a description is good and valid. But in Asia, we share life and struggle with followers of many religions or of none. It will be helpful here to have, in addition to this description, another which will be universal and comprehensive. In Asia, it is necessary for us to ask: How would a Buddhist describe spirituality? or a Muslim, a Hindu, or even a Marxist?

Spirituality has been further described as life rendered into a pilgrimage by the Holy Spirit. Or as the relation of our spirit to the Spirit of God. Or again, as the inward journey, including conversion, personal discipline, and worship in community. Or finally, spirituality has been described as desert experience. Or as living and walking in God's presence with body and mind and soul in the midst of the sufferings and struggles of this world.[4]

All these descriptions are precious. They include the inner dynamism which impels life; they include values which orient it, and the lifestyle in which the dynamism and the values find concrete expression. It is also valid and poetic to see life as a pilgrimage led by the Spirit who never allows us to strike roots on the road, to make our home in past or present achievements, but impels us forward to the yet-to-be, through a divine discontent which uproots us continually.

But what is the historical goal of such a pilgrimage? And is there no outward journey into a world and a history to be liberated, transformed, and brought to wholeness? What does walking with God mean in concrete history and day-to-day life? And how do we distinguish the voice of God whom we follow from the many voices of today's idols? At any rate, these fine descriptions are religious still, while in Asia and in today's pluralistic world, we need to speak of a secular spirituality as well.

Some of the major partial liberations carried out in Asia are the outcome of distinctively secular aspirations and secular efforts.

The Meaning of Spirituality in Asia

At this point, we need to reflect on the very word "spirituality." The word is problematic: it seems to exclude *a priori* all material reality and activities bound up with matter and its processes. It suggests the immaterial, the interior, the other-worldly, and so forth. The difficulty arises from the Greek understanding of the spirit as superior to matter, as incorruptible, as wholly other than matter. The Christian tradition should therefore trace its way back to the Hebrew *ruah*, the breath of God, the wind of God, the energy and the power of God. Spiritual life is human life, the whole of human life inspired and led by the Spirit, the energizing presence and activity of God. That avoids docetism, individualism, dualism, and elitism.

The Spirit is the breath of God by which we breathe. It is the divine sea of life in which we live and move and have our being. A sense of being immersed in the divine and suffused by the Spirit is an essential component of Asian-ness. It liberates us from shallow secularism, from reductionist rationalism and scientism. It saves us also from a concept of God who is entirely outside and has then to be imposed upon us. "This whole universe is permeated by the Lord," says the Isavasya Upanishad. This sense of the Spirit has given to Asia the ability to see things as symbols and to intuit the Divine as the depth reality of things. For Asia the Spirit is transcendent in its immanence. The Spirit is the Self. It is the ultimate Self of every self. The Spirit is the one "I," the rest of reality being in the third person, being created, thing, or object: they are he, she or it, until they are called, named, and spoken to by God the Spirit who thereby constitutes the creature, the he, the she, and the it into "thou" and "you."

But the Spirit is also action and freedom, energy and movement, and life and justice. And therefore the Spirit is struggle against all that contradicts, obstructs, restricts, or destroys freedom, life, and love. The Spirit is the spirit of combat. It is thus that the Spirit has been experienced by the masses whose stories are told in the Bible, in the Koran, in the Puranas of India, in the anecdotes, dances, and paintings of the minjung. It is thus that people experience the Spirit today, as a new sense of and aspiration for freedom; as readiness to act and take risks—a readiness that is surprising and humanly inexplicable; as the new voice people have found with which to protest, to demand, and to affirm as never before; as fresh appreciation of the gift of life and its beauty and its preciousness which they are ready to nurture and to protect; and finally, as community, in which through cooperation and sacrificial love people find their authentic self and the power and promise of their future.

The Spirit of God is experienced today by the masses of the people as action and combat, articulate and distinct, in defense of shared freedom and life in community. The experience of the Spirit

> has one single object, God and creation united. It is experience of God in creation and creation in God. It is experience of God as acting on us and on the world at the same time, relating us to the world and the world to us, not in some vague cosmic contact but in a specific and limited course of action. There is no separation between the experience of acting and the experience of the Spirit who acts, between experiencing the Spirit and experiencing "me" and "us." ... In the same way, there is no separation between action and prayer, practice in the world and celebration of the practice.[5]

Thus the word "spiritual" can be profoundly meaningful and quite acceptable to all religious traditions. It can also be acceptable to Marxists, or at least to Marxians, since it occurs occasionally in Karl Marx's writings to indicate the authenticity and the depth of the human.

But the smell of Greek philosophy still clings to the word "spiritual." Many people are uncomfortable with "spirituality" despite the fact that youth from the affluent capitalist West, tired of the superficiality and banality of consumerism, turn to Asia in search of what is traditionally called spirituality. George Soares Prabhu, therefore, would suggest the word *dharma* for the word "spirituality." *Dharma* is central to Hindu and Buddhist traditions. I would, however, suggest a simpler definition or description in very ordinary words, people's words. This description is at once comprehensive and universal, yet represents the heart of the matter. It is dynamic and historical, holistic and avoids dichotomy. In it the part we play—we have to play— is accented, and God's part is presupposed and understood. For God's presence and activity, while basic, remain mysterious and hidden all the while and noiseless, like the engine of a good automobile.

Spirituality as Response-ability

I suggest, then, that spirituality be understood and described in terms of two related ideas or realities or activities, namely, openness and response-ability. I write response-ability with a hyphen in order not to restrict its meaning to accountability. To be spiritual is to be ever more open and response-able to reality. This calls for some clarification.

Reality here refers to everything—from sand and stone and the earth, through grass and trees, through worms and birds and their songs, through human beings, their lives, their history, on to the ultimate Mystery we call God. The more open we are, the more spiritual; the more realities to which we are open, the greater the spirituality; the greater the depths and the profounder the meanings of reality to which we are open, the more authentic the spirituality. The more significant the reality to which we make ourselves open, the finer the spirituality that is lived. Thus, for instance, the questions of ecology, of human rights and freedoms, of food for the masses, of work, of the suffering of the people, are of far greater significance and weight than the idiosyncrasies and luxuries of the rich few.

Openness means letting reality, significant for personal and social life and for the health of the earth, come and invade, enter, affect, disturb, challenge, mold and move us to joy, to tears, to anger, to action. It means contemplation, listening to reality, to things and to events, listening to their voices and messages as well as their silences. Nature as well as history can be contemplated. And history can be Bible history, as in traditional monastic contemplation. But history can, must, also be contemporary history, our history. For salvation history is the depth mystery of human history. Contemplation seeks to discern where — in what flowers, birds, events, crosses, and uprisings — God is now present and active to save. We discern this so that we may hasten to stand by God and become God's coworkers.

Contemplation and action are interlinked. There are three types or models of this relationship. One is distributive: some persons choose a contemplative style of life, others choose an active lifestyle.

The second is an alternating model, that is, the same person is now active and then contemplative, both for considerable periods of time. The third is interpenetrative. This means we all act and reflect most of the time. This last seems to be the biblical model, the *Gita* model, the actual model discernible in the daily life of people everywhere, of workers, housewives, children, artists, architects. Historically, even the religious movements seem to be heading toward an interpenetrative style where contemplation and action go together.

Openness includes cultivating awareness of the depth and mystery of things, events, and people. Things are not mere surface realities. Things have depth and hidden meanings. They are in fact words of God, ways in which God is disclosing God's heart and saying something to us. So is every human person, every human face, and all human relationships marked by justice, reverence, and love. That is why things and persons are symbols and sacraments. This is an Asian view and an Asian sense of reality. It is the basis of sacramental representations and symbolic celebrations, as well as of poetry and art. This poetic, symbolic approach to reality is integral to the human heart. Only the shallowness of rationalist science, consumerism, and a commodity culture has all but killed the symbolic and the poetic in many an affluent part of the world. In Asia, the language of poetry and symbol and the language and poetry of the body and of material things must continue to be an essential part of our spirituality.

Another act of openness is the readiness to study reality, to analyze it, and understand it in depth. Social realities in particular are complex and intricate. To contemplate them is to study them analytically and historically. Such contemplation will reveal the possibility and the actuality of different perspectives on reality.

One can consider a boat tossed by a stormy sea from the top of a hill, or from within the storm-beaten boat. From the hilltop, everything may look beautiful and romantic; one may stand there and write a poem. Within the boat the experience is mortal fear and agony. Reality can be seen from the perspective of those at the top: the rich, the powerful, and the privileged; or of those at the bottom: the poor, the oppressed, the victims of the system. To stand on the hilltop and surrender to poetic fancy is not openness to reality. The reality is the threat of death that the occupants of the boat are facing and the fear that grips them. Spirituality consists in being open to this reality, in being alive enough to sense its possibility, and in coming down from the hill to enter the waters and do all that is possible, even at risk to ourselves, to bring help to the men and women in danger of death. Spirituality is to adopt the perspective of the poor, the marginalized, and the disempowered victims of the established system.

Openness, therefore, includes discernment, evaluation, and criticism: criticism of society, of economic policies, political spheres, religions, churches, theologies, and traditional spiritualities. Critical activity is often considered incompatible with spirituality. It seems that critical study of the Bible has shaken the faith of certain people. That may be true of arrogant criticism that is abstract and academic. The criticism we are talking of is the exercise of discernment which consists in raising questions about the service to life, dignity, and faith that doctrines, interpretations, scholarship, churches, governments, laws, scientific research, medical systems, developmental models, and so on, can and do render. If they render little or no service to life and faith, they are surely incompatible with the openness we are considering. True criticism really comes from the Bible itself, from life's concrete needs and situations, and from the poor. To raise questions from their perspective, and so continually to evaluate and judge the meaningfulness and relevance of things, is the openness that defines spirituality.

May we consider the open arms and the open heart of the crucified Jesus as symbols of his spirituality? God's skies and

God's seas are open. God's flowers open in the morning—symbols of the spirituality of God. God is open to our world and is affected by everything that happens here.

Response-ability consists in our willingness and readiness to respond to significant realities and situations of import for life. It is complete only in the actual giving of the response. Openness is already a type of response. Further openness and response consists in acting to transform reality. One denounces, rejects, and resists whatever is alienating, death dealing, and dehumanizing. One announces, nurtures, and constructs what makes for fuller life, for finer humanity, and for a new earth. Response includes acting to change awareness and attitudes, and acting to change structures both of the heart and of society.

Response-ability thus implies conversion. Conversion is more than repentance and change in the secret recesses of the heart. It is other than a transfer of allegiance from one religious group or institution to another. Conversion consists in a fundamental change of perspective, in beginning to see reality with new eyes: with and through the eyes of the least and the deprived, which are the eyes of Jesus Christ, the eyes of God. The *Bhagavad Gita* holds that to see reality our fleshly (self-regarding) eyes have to be replaced by the "divine eye" which is Krishna's gracious gift. The New Testament describes conversion in terms of a radical symbol of new birth. To convert is to leave the old road and walk a new one, to take a new direction, to begin to live differently, to identify with the cause and the struggles of the poor.

In our concrete world, conversion would consist in turning from the views and ways of exploiters and oppressors, conquerors and colonialists; in turning from the race for private wealth and the competition to grab power in order to control people and use them; in turning from the ideology of capitalism with its individualism, atheism, and militarism, its consumerism and commodity culture that degrades everything, including human beings, their labor power and their sexuality, to the status of merchandise, and measures people's worth by counting the fetishes they have accumulated. Conversion would also consist in turning from the developmental models that the capitalist West sells to Asia and that our westernized elite buy—models that only continue and deepen our dependence and impede the unfolding of Asian initiatives and the clarification of Asian vision of life and life's true destiny; and in turning from the idolatry of Western science and technology that become hegemonic and violent, pollute the earth, and kill life. Conversion would mean a return to the primacy of the human whom God loves, and to the task of receiving our authentic Asian identities, of redefining development as if people mattered, and of reshaping economic and political life on the basis of equality, dignity, freedom, and food for all.

Many a situation in Asia is fraught with threat and danger. To respond to these situations is to take risks and become vulnerable. It is to this dangerous living that our faith, any authentic faith, commits us. Faith is not a search for security, for infallible authority, or for ready-made definitions and lifestyles. Faith is commitment to Mystery and to the Central Darkness from which all light comes; it is stepping into the Unknown. A faith of that kind, transcending the ideology of security, is implied in today's responses to situations of oppression. It is embodied in the life of the numberless martyrs of our day, who, in most Asian lands, have been or are being harassed, jailed, tortured, and killed because they stand for human rights and justice to the poor and freedom and food for all.

Spirituality and Poverty

I would like to illustrate the description of spirituality given above by relating it to one of the major significant realities of our continent, namely, the massive poverty of our people, which is widespread and deep and causes misery to hundreds of millions of children, women, and men. There exist three levels of openness to the reality of poverty, three types of understanding it, three modes of awareness. One considers poverty as natural, as part of the human condition, as the result of *karma* or fate, or the disposition of divine providence, as St. Pius X once wrote.

The second looks on poverty as the product of Asia's (and Africa's and Latin America's) failure to bring about revolutions in thought, philosophy, technology, and social organization. The failure is called backwardness. These continents, therefore, are a few centuries behind Europe, which carried out these revolutions and went ahead of the rest.

A third understanding of poverty denies that the misery of the people is the work of nature, fate, or providence. It denies the theory of backwardness and its presuppositions, and points out the suppression of the major factors that made (Western) Europe rich, namely, imperialism, world conflict, colonial destruction of great cultures and flourishing economies, the plunder of the colonies and transfer of wealth to the West, deep exploitation of the colonies' human and natural resources, slave trade and forced labor, sea piracy and wars among the robbers themselves, organized terrorism and violence, and massive genocide. It further emphasizes the fact that many of the countries that are now "backward" and "underdeveloped" were, before the eruption of colonial imperialism, far ahead of Western Europe in industry, technology, and wealth, in social organization and culture, in philosophy and thought. Hence, in analyzing the reality of poverty factually and historically, this third type of analysis views poverty as the product of injustice and oppression. Recall the telltale title of one of Walter Rodney's books: *How Europe Under-developed Africa.*

To these three approaches to and interpretation of poverty correspond three distinct types of response. The first response is that poverty is natural, or assigned by fate, or willed by God. It cannot be abolished; nothing radical can be done about it. All we can do is to alleviate the suffering it causes, give alms, dress a few wounds, and wipe a few tears. Most religions and churches are familiar with this response. They are deeply marked by it.

To the second type of analysis, namely, the theory and ideology of backwardness, the response is that of modernization: follow the West, accumulate capital, invest, industrialize, produce, consume. If need be, borrow money, borrow technology. Wealth and prosperity will abound at the top of the social pyramid, and will trickle down by and by to the masses below who have, in the meantime, been exploited, squeezed, and broken to produce that prosperity. This is the response of capitalist ideology. It is accepted by most governments and colonially educated elite in the Asian countries despite the ample factual evidence that the trickle-down does not happen. In this system, the flow of wealth is always one way, with the result that the rich grow richer and the poor become poorer. The day the exploiting and squeezing of the poor slackens, the system begins to totter and develops leaks.

To the third type of analysis that considers poverty as injustice, the response is action to change the system, to dismantle the structures of exploitation, to decolonize our minds, and to redefine life's ways and goals. Opting for a human culture in place of today's dominant money culture, we seek to envision another kind of social order, a different organization of economic life and of other types of relationships that is marked by equality and freedom for all to be creative and caring. Frantz Fanon's observation is pertinent here. If all we want is to make Asia a (carbon) copy of Western Europe, why did we send the Europeans away? Call them back. They can do this job far better than we can. They are adept in impersonal technology. They only fail when human beings have to be taken into account. To build a human culture, let us cease aping and fashion new ideas and new ways of doing things.

These three types of openness and response represent kinds of spirituality. The first is the spirituality of relief, the second the spirituality of reform, and the third the spirituality of liberation. The spirituality of relief is what the religions and churches have always lived. Today it is conspicuously represented by Mother Teresa of India and supported by the rich of the world. The spirituality of reform retains the old framework of social, economic, and power relations and leaves the main features of the landscape undisturbed. It only rearranges, repaints, and renames the furniture. No new directions and dynamisms are introduced. The spirituality of liberation works for radical change in the set up of human existence and relationships. The criterion for change is the promise that change carries of fuller life, finer humanity, and a new earth.

Conclusion

The spirituality of liberation could be further illustrated with many a biblical story. Exodus, for instance, opens with a description of reality: the pharaoh's policies and the condition of the people. The situation is analyzed from the viewpoint of the victims and understood as oppression. The response is resistance and revolt, initiated by a group of women, picked up by Moses, and carried on by the whole people as a struggle of liberation till they fight their way into freedom and the beginning of a new future. This response was their liberation spirituality, which they crowned with the joyful liturgy in dance, song, and memory (Exodus 15).

The "Our Father" is an expression of liberation spirituality as well as a program of action for liberation. At its heart is the earth. The prayer and the striving is that it may happen on the earth and to the earth. God should happen to the earth, and God's will should. The Kingdom of God should happen to it. And a meaningful name of God should happen to it. This magnificent dream or utopia is then spelled out in concrete historical terms by naming bread/rice for every child, woman, and man every day. The word about food for all is followed by a word about forgiveness. The unexpressed logic of it seems to be that in our present situation of unequal distribution of the earth and its resources, action to set right the imbalance and the injustice cannot but be conflictual. And conflicts are not finally resolved and humanized except in mutual and abounding pardon and forgiveness. Both our conflict and our peace are horizoned within the larger and more original reality of God's own forgiving love. The spirituality of the "Our Father" is liberational.

In conclusion, let me refer to the spirituality of Gitanjali as it finds expression in her poems. Gitanjali was born in Meerut, India, on June 12, 1961; she died of cancer in Bombay on August 11, 1977, shortly after her sixteenth birthday. After Gitanjali's death her mother discovered her poems written on pieces of paper and hidden away under the mattress, behind books and sofa seats, inside cushion covers, and in little corners of her room at home and in the hospital. Gitanjali knew her life was brief, but she did not want her mother to know this. Her poems have been collected and published, their grammar and spelling left unaltered. In them this child meets the terror of death as well as death's promises. She gives expression to her deep love for life and to her hurt, pain, and sorrow as life was being taken from her. She has faith in God whom she also questions, Job-like: why should this happen to her who is so young, who loves life so deeply, and who has never hurt anyone? She fights her fate while also accepting it.

The poems are the voice of her suffering and intense loneliness, and are remarkably free of any sense of despair. From her bed of pain she contemplates the beauty of trees, seeks to comfort others and spare them, and remembers the dog she left behind, Moti, her friend, and prays that someone may give him a rug when the rains come, and that he may find a friend to care for him lest he be "shivering with lack of love." After reading the poems of Gitanjali tearfully, I ask myself: From where come this vision of life, this great wisdom, this faith and love, this courage to face pain and death and "the dark of the unknown," this depth of spirit, and this strength of character? And this complete openness to her situation, and this moving response so clear, so discerning, and so human? They come from the spirit of Asia; they are Asia's gift to a child of Asia.

Notes

1. Also known in Asia as Kim Ji Ha, Kim Chi Ha is a Catholic Korean poet and prophet who was arrested in 1970 for a poem satirizing government corruption. A charismatic person who did much of his writing in prison, he was nominated in 1975 for the Nobel Prize in both Peace and Literature.

2. Quoted by Melanio La Guardia Aoanan, "From Story Telling to Social Transformation: Theologizing through Peoples' Movements," in Yeow Choo Lak, ed., *Doing Theology and Peoples' Movements in Asia* (n.p., 1987).

3. John W. Lewis and Kathleen J. Hartford, *Peasant Rebellion and Communist Revolution in Asia* (Stanford, Calif.: Stanford University Press, 1974), 3.

4. World Council of Churches, "Spiritual Formation in Theological Education. An Invitation to Participation" (Iona Document, 1987).

5. José Comblin, *Holy Spirit and Liberation* (Maryknoll, N.Y.: Orbis Books, 1988), 31.

3

Liberating Spirituality in the Korean Minjung Tradition

Shamanism and Minjung Liberation

David Kwang-sun Suh

Since the early 1970s, a handful of Korean theologians have become interested in Korean shamanism, which is probably the most basic and pervasive form of Korean religiosity or spirituality. Until then, shamanism had been regarded as the enemy of Christianity and was categorically rejected by the missionaries as idol worship. Conversion to Christ meant throwing away all the ways of Korean shamanism, which was considered to be nothing but superstitious belief in spirits in trees and stones and in all other living and non-living things.

In the past, if missionaries did study Korean shamanism, it was approached as a subject of comparative religion or in the interest of evangelistic conversion. More recently, Korean shamanism has been studied by Christian theologians who are interested in the process of the indigenization of Christianity. After all, shamanism is part of what may be called the religious "soil" of Korea. Nevertheless, in spite of the missionaries' efforts to reject shamanism and to guard Christianity against it, Korean Christianity has been "shamanized." Christianity has taken deep roots in the indigenous Korean religiosity and has become strong and vital. The vitality of Korean Christianity has been known as a success story of Christian mission in the "non-Christian" world.

But the question has been raised: Is shamanized Korean Christianity compatible with the gospel of Jesus? This is a basic question but it is also a risky question. It is tantamount to asking whether Korean Christianity is real Christianity. In other words, can we find a liberating spirituality in Korean Christianity, a Christianity that is deeply shamanized?

Korean shamanism is basically a family-centered religion that conserves the welfare of the family by exorcising the evil spirits, healing the sick in the family, and taking care of the ancestor spirits and the deceased. In the shamanistic mentality, religion is to relate oneself in peace and harmony with the spirits in and around the house, living and dead, in order to preserve the well-being of the members of the family and to promote the health, wealth, and success of the household.

As Korean shamanism is individualistic, family-centered, and conservative, and interested in health, wealth, success, and blessings, so shamanized Korean Christianity is basically individualistic and conservative, interested in the material blessings and successes of this world as well as of the next. When one realizes that Korean Christianity has been shamanized, then what becomes of the liberating aspect of the gospel of Jesus? To borrow the phrase and concern of Dietrich Bonhoeffer, do we have to advocate a non-religious or non-shamanistic interpretation of Korean Christianity? In other words, in order to find Korean Christianity liberating, must we "de-shamanize" Korean Christianity? From a liberational point of view, would the shamanistic elements in Korean Christianity have to be rooted out and rejected in order to sustain a liberating spirituality?

Thus comes the crisis of the theology of indigenization: indigenized Korean Christianity is strong and dynamic, but is it not against the liberating gospel of Jesus Christ? Does it mean giving up on our theological efforts to understand and dialogue with other indigenous religions? What, in fact, shall we do about the acculturation and indigenization of the Christian gospel in Asian and Korean culture? Are we to deny and condemn Korean shamanism and shamanized Christianity altogether? To use H. Richard Niebuhr's typology, are we to go against culture as our missionaries did?

Confronting this critical dilemma, Korean minjung theologians discovered anew that Korean shamanism is the religion of the people — the poor, oppressed, and socially marginalized. The shaman rituals are performed to cure the sick, to comfort the lost ones, and to reconcile broken families. Shamans even feed and make happy the unhappy wandering spirits of the deceased which have no place to settle for good. The minjung are *han*-ridden people. *Han* can be described as the feeling of anger of the people brought about by injustice inflicted upon them. However, it is not merely a psychological state, but also political and economic realities interacting and bringing themselves to bear on the mind and body of the minjung. Thus the minjung live with *han*, they accumulate *han*, and they die with *han*.

If shamanism performs the priestly function of comforting the *han*-ridden minjung, it should be the role of shamanized Korean minjung Christianity to comfort *han*-ridden people and release their *han*. This leads to forgiveness of sin, and it is a liberative act. The late minjung theologian Suh Nam Dong put it this way:

> The priestly function is not to give comfort to the rich and the powerful and bless their oppressive power and exploitation. It is not to hypnotize the oppressed and put their resistance forces to sleep. Truly, it is the job of the priests to take care of the wounds of the minjung and enable them to restore their self-respect and courage, and to respond to their historical aspirations. This is to resolve their *han*. This is to comfort the *han*-ridden hearts of the people. (My translation from Korean.)

The spirituality of minjung is a spirituality which has risen out of deep feelings of *han*. Minjung spirituality is to overcome the *han* of an individual as well as the collective *han* of the people. Minjung spirituality is the crying and moaning of the *han*-ridden spirits of the people, the poor, and the oppressed to God. It is thus a liberating spirituality: it is a crying out for liberation and a struggle for liberation from the *han* creating political oppression and economic exploitation. Minjung spirituality deeply imbedded in Korean shamanism is a combat spirituality.

Out of this spirituality, one of the mothers of young activist Christian students imprisoned during the democratization movement of the 1970s prays:

> We cannot keep back our tears. Since there is no way to still the sorrow in our hearts, we have wandered around lonely mountain-tops crying aloud to you. And we have had night-long prayer vigils putting our plea before you in tears. Now, O God, delay no longer, but take pity on us and answer our prayers.

Our mothers' spirituality is different from shamanized religiosity. Our mothers do not pray for selfish blessings, success, or protection; they cry out for justice and liberation. Furthermore, they articulate their sons' participation in the spirituality of liberation in the following prayer:

> O God, examine our sons' hearts. They did not put pleasure or happiness first, but truly loved their neighbors. . . . They followed God's word; they were honest and they despised injustice; they knew how to distinguish truth from falsehood and helped many to realize God's love. They truly made an effort to live love. . . . We cannot but give thanks to God when we hear of their having shared even a piece of bread with others in prison. O God, have mercy on them. . . .

The spirituality of minjung would not give in to the oppressive feelings of *han*. It is to fight against the oppressive structure of *han*. Indeed, the spirituality of minjung is a combat spirituality.

It is against this background of minjung spirituality that we can appreciate the shaman ritual of *gut* described in greater detail in the following section. Lee Chung Hee brings out clearly the liberational spirituality in the practice of the shaman ritual of *gut*. He stresses the collective nature of the village community shaman rituals and the lively festival which follows. The *gut* is the place where the people become a community, whole and united, and re-create their energy to labor and love. When *gut* is performed in a village community, it is not constrained by individual greed, nor is it a merely "religious" affair. Rather, it is open to the world and to the community for peace, justice, and well-being. This is "secular spirituality."

What moves the *gut* and is at the same time created by the *gut* is the life force that Lee calls the *shin-myung*. It is the spirituality that the minjung in the village *gut* experience, and participate and share in. The term *shin-myung* may be translated into English as "divine excitement" for "*shin*" in a Chinese character means "heaven" or "divine" and "*myung*" stands for "brightness." *Shin-myung* is not necessarily a religious feeling, but rather a highly spirited feeling, a creative dynamism flowing out of one's viscera. It is a *gut*-level feeling of strength for life, a feeling of the body, and not of the soul separate from the body. Thus, it would be more accurate to say that this is the life force that makes a person integrated and whole, with a sound mind and healthy body. Lee points out that the *shin-myung*, the spirituality of minjung experienced and shared in the village community, is in the very life of the minjung, in their love for one another and in their labor together with one another. There would be no spirituality of minjung outside of their life, and labor, their struggle for life, and their experience of love.

The problem now is that since the Japanese colonial government for decades suppressed the village shaman rituals as a subversive act of resistance, and since the dictatorial governments opposed the revival of the minjung *gut* movement as a subversive means of struggle, its actual tradition has been uprooted and is dying out in our village communities. Our task remains, however, with Korean Christianity. Shamanized Korean Christianity should revive and revitalize the liberating spirituality of minjung. We do not have to "de-shamanize" Korean Christianity but "re-shamanize" it. That is, the liberating gospel of Jesus Christ should be indigenized into the minjung spirituality of Korean shaman tradition. In this way, the liberating tradition of minjung spirituality in Korean shamanism could transform shamanized Korean Christianity. At the same time, this liberating spirituality of Jesus Christ could transform shamanized Korean Christianity for the mission of God in the world.

Historically, we can say that the Farmers' Rebellion in 1894 was a political movement of the minjung for justice, stimulated and mobilized by a new religion, the Eastern Learning (*Dong-hak* in Korean). *Dong-hak*, as an indigenous religious movement, attempted to integrate Korean traditional religions such as Confucianism, Buddhism, and shamanism. It is remarkable how this awakening of traditional religious spirituality mobilized an intense political movement of the farmers' struggle against the powers-that-be. The Korean farmers have found a liberating spirituality in the traditional Korean religions. It is this spirituality of minjung that was rediscovered and shared by them. It is this spirituality that makes the oppressed minjung believe that they are the subjects of history and liberation.

We must remind ourselves that the Korean people have been blessed with rich and diverse religious traditions besides shamanism, including Confucianism and Buddhism. Therefore, searching for a liberation spirituality in Korean Christianity, we must investigate the liberational aspects of these traditional Korean religions. A Korean Christian spirituality cannot be formulated or nurtured apart from these rich and profound sources of spirituality.

Questions should be raised as to the nature of Confucian, Buddhist, and shaman spiritualities and their contributions to the formation and transformation of Christian spirituality. However, I have focused on shamanism in order to discover the ways in which this religious tradition contributes to our search for an indigenous and liberating Korean Christian spirituality. In this search it is crucial to have a clear and correct understanding of the *dae-dong gut* and *shin-myung*, both vital for a proper interpretation of shamanism.

Liberation Spirituality in Dae-dong Gut

Lee Chung Hee

Recent Korean minjung theological writings have taken into serious account elements in shamanism. However, these writings have usually confined their focus to the "dissolution of *han*" in the shaman ritual of the *gut*. As a cult performed by shamans, the *gut* is generally understood as a ritual offering to the gods on behalf of the dead. Because the priests of *han* have not been able to reflect the *gut* in the communal life of the minjung, it becomes necessary to redefine *gut* and to come to a new consciousness of it — that it is a cult not for the soul confronted by unrighteous death, but for the living. The *gut* is precisely for the liberation of the minjung — the poor, oppressed, and marginalized people who labor and love. This presentation approaches the rites of *gut* from this perspective — that *gut* is for the living and not for the dead.

This section focuses on the liberating spirituality within the tradition of the Korean minjung, rather than on doing theology as such. The work of theologizing on this theme is yet another task.

Understanding *Dae-dong Gut*

To begin with, we need a more discriminating or nuanced understanding of *gut*. As a Korean word, *gut* is used to express both festival and ritual. Therefore, *gut* was a main medium by which traditional minjung culture was created and continued.

The traditional *gut* can be either an individual or a village *gut*, depending on the subject or character of the ritual. In the category of individual *gut*, there are basically three kinds: one that seeks the cure of illnesses; one that asks for blessings upon a family; and one that serves as initiation rite or as ritual on behalf of victims of unjust deaths. Unlike the individual *gut* which varies according to purpose, the village *gut* differs according to the region in which it is performed. In every village *gut*, the subjects are generally all residents of the village, and the *gut* is directly linked to the community life of a given region. Ideologically, the village *gut* is a community ritual that integrates communal work and play, so that it is generally accompanied by village meetings and communal play. In some regions, the *gut* is directed by a *nong-ak* (farm music) band, where the players use traditional Korean musical instruments, including gongs and cymbals. Thus the *gut* is an integral part of the culture of the minjung that nurtures their communal life energy, that is, their *shin-myung.*

While traditionally a village *gut* received its name according to the region of origin, in today's *gut* movement there is a particular *gut* referred to simply as *dae-dong gut* (literally "Great Togetherness Festival") in accordance with its ideological form. While it is relatively easy to deduce the origins of the names of the various village *gut* by tracing the nature of the deity, sacred building, seasonal festivals, or the core of the *gut*'s content, it is difficult to discern the origins of the title *dae-dong* because of its strong ideological character. The closest approximation as to its origin might be the idea of the Confucianist Utopia which appears in the Chinese classic.

There are a number of features of the *dae-dong gut* performed by the village community. Unlike seasonal festivals and peasant rituals, the *dae-dong gut* is carried out annually, or even every five or ten years, depending on the circumstances of the village. Traditionally, the Korean minjung performed festive rituals on a monthly basis. Because the subjects of the village *gut* are all of the village residents, the shaman is in charge of only one part of the *gut.*

There are two types of village *gut.* The first type is performed by a shaman and calls for the participation of all the village residents in the sacred place. The second is performed by the *nong-ak* band that travels from house to house in the village. At either *gut*, the village residents select the leader, someone in the village whose family has not been subjected to misfortune or unlucky omens.

The sacred symbol of the village is often a tree or stone, although some shrines are erected inside mountains. Trees considered sacred are often old trees in the village. During the performance of *gut*, one tree is selected as the sacred tree possessing the spirit. It is cut and erected in the area where the *gut* is to take place. At that precise moment, the area is transformed into a sacred place. A few days prior to the performance of the *gut*, clean ocher is spread over the area in order to consecrate it, and a rim of straw is used to border off this area.

The deity worshiped in the *dae-dong gut* is of various types. One of these is the village god connected to the legendary founding of the village. There are other deities, including nameless gods of the heavens, earth, rivers, and the ocean; souls which have died unjust deaths in natural calamities or in historical events; and historical or legendary figures who have become deified.

In the *gut* performed by villagers near the seashore, the last rite is similar to expelling a scapegoat. This last rite consists of making a straw model ship on which food is placed and cast off to sea. This rite signifies the expulsion of all evil spirits and disaster which cause calamity upon the living.

A *dae-dong gut* is a grand festival that takes up to one month of preparation and may last for as many as ten days. As part of the process, the village people hold a *dae-dong* council. This council selects the village representatives, discusses ways of raising funds for the village, and deliberates on the ways of distributing the communal labor. The profits from communal labor are used for the benefit of the whole village: for example, for the repair of village roads or for acquiring *nong-ak* instruments.

In addition to the *dae-dong* council, *dae-dong* play (akin to fun and games) is also part of the *dae-dong gut. Dae-dong* play cultivates the communal spirit within the village and forms the basis for the creation and development of minjung cultural art. The play, led by *nong-ak*, includes tug-of-war, mask dances, stone battles, and wrestling, and integrates an acute sense of critique and an intense spirit of battle. Similar to the medieval Western European "Feast of Fools," it is a form of chaos that re-creates the life force.

The subject, the energy, and the life force which lead the *dae-dong gut* are not the deity, the spirit of dead souls, or the shaman; it is the spirit of the minjung which lives amid the communal village — the *shin-myung* that, as said before, not only directs the *dae-dong gut*, but is also created through the *dae-dong gut*.

Understanding *Shin-myung* as a Spirituality of Minjung

Shin-myung is that burst of energy that allows the crippled to dance and that springs out through the dance. It expands and touches all the other people in the *ma-dang* (village square) so that they also rise up to dance. *Shin-myung* is not an abstract concept but a word that is deeply connected with the realities of life and the will for life itself. In Korean, the expression *"shin-nan-da"* (literally "divine wind") is often used. This expression refers to a life that is worth living, a life full of vitality, joy, and wonder. The *shin-myung* influence in minjung religion is great.

Phenomenologically, what we refer to when we say *"shin-nan-da"* is the advent of the *shin-myung* within a community or individual so that we are filled with a vitality for life. It is therefore different from religious ecstasy. Of course, we also use the word *shin-myung* to denote the possession of spirit or the psychological state of possession in traditional Korean shamanism. In the study of Korean shamanism, this *shin-myung* is differentiated in terms of individual and community *shin-myung*. Individual *shin-myung* refers to the state when the shaman alone is possessed by the spirit. But more important is when this individually possessed *shin-myung* extends to reach the whole of the community. When the shaman alone is in possession of the spirit, the *shin-myung* is deified through the shaman, but when it enters the community, the deification is sublimated into a communal life force and vitality. In other words, religious *shin-myung* is transformed into the *shin-ba-ram* (divine wind) of life.

The state and place in which the *shin-ba-ram* explodes within the community is similar to the collective ecstasy in the religious context. But the Korean *dae-dong gut* reveals other characteristics as well. The human sanctification, the destruction, and the expulsion of the libido through collective ecstasy must be reexamined from the perspective of Korean minjung *gut*. In other words, *shin-myung* is not simply a religious phenomenon or a phenomenon that appears through rapport with a transcending world; it must be related to the life and realities of the minjung. The *shin-myung* in the *dae-dong gut* shatters the existing system of values and order through the prayers and struggles of the minjung who seek a new world order. The *shin-myung* is the transforming force of individuals and society. And it is a spirituality of the Korean minjung that is expressed anew in a Christian spirituality of liberation.

The philosophical and theoretical grounds regarding *shin-myung* can be found in the works of Kim Ji Ha. Though it might be repetitive, I would like to examine briefly the discourse by Kim Ji Ha regarding this topic.

Kim Ji Ha's discourse on *shin-myung* is aphoristic, which demands a great power of imagination from the readers. When he refers to *shin-myung*, it is always in a collective and communal sense. To Kim Ji Ha, *shin-myung* is "life."

> *Shin-myung* is precisely the subject and basis of work and dance. Without *shin-myung*, we could neither work nor dance. Without it, work is like forced slave labor. Without it, dance would be a dance of compulsion. Physical and mental labor are originally one and are forms of activity of one life force. Likewise, art and labor are the activities of one life force. They are the activities of the *shin-myung*.[1]

This *shin-myung* is "a communal force which springs from unknown sources." Therefore, communal *shin-myung* is life itself, but this does not refer simply to the survival of life. It is a resistance "to being killed," and the power of living is a liberating life. This *shin-myung* always springs forth to confront the power of "being killed" and is also the freedom that strengthens the volition for life. Through this process, the *shin-myung* expands its strength further, allows one to participate in liberating work and play, and integrates work and play into the *shin-myung*. Kim Ji Ha says the following: "The *shin-myung* is the concrete form of freedom in action. It is the enhanced activities of the life force which creates, liberates, and unites the life of the minjung by minjung themselves." In the end, the *shin-myung* is "enhanced fulfillment of the life energy" that transforms all forces of killing and liberates life toward a newer and greater life.

Kim Ji Ha refers to *shin-myung* in its totality as "the *élan vital* of life in the living" and "the *élan vital* of life which makes human beings live life as human beings." It is precisely this *élan vital* that springs from human life and overcomes the dualistic conflicts of human life (between the soul and body, matter and mind, individual and society, speech and action) to make human beings live healthy human lives. "If a person is without sickness, division, alienation, hate, and isolation, then the *shin-myung* within this person is said to be productively, reconciliatorily, and actively living within this person."

This understanding of life/*shin-myung* by Kim Ji Ha is directly linked to the concept of *gut*. To Kim Ji Ha, *gut* is that which "partly ties the beginning and end of the process of expanding and reproducing the activities of life, capable of sublimating work into play and play into work." To put it more plainly, the *gut* of the Korean people, and in particular, the peasants, is "an event which calls together the *shin-myung*, and with this, exorcises all of the evil spirits which cause calamity upon the people." *Gut* functions as a calling of the *shin-myung*. Through the power of the *shin-myung*, the *gut* casts away the evil spirits that are responsible for all sorts of evil and evil actions, calamities, unhappiness, sicknesses, ruptures between human beings that divide minds and create confusion, exploit the fruits of labor and monopolize them, and cause the minjung to suffer starvation.

Finally, Kim Ji Ha reveals to us one other important fact regarding the *shin-myung*. This fact is connected to the relationship between *shin-myung* and minjung art. Korean minjung theology, through study of the mask dance, has already reflected a part of this fact in its theological works. The *shin-myung* as critical transcendence in minjung art does not appear only in the form of a blood-thirsty wrath. Rather it is bittersweet and humorous, possesses wit and composure as well as sharp satirical presence. At the same time, it is revealed as firm and sly resistance as well as attack. The *shin-myung* embraces all life, calls it to reconciliation and unity, and expands it.

In summary, the *dae-dong gut* of the minjung aims at the regeneration and expansion of the life force. Through this *gut*, the minjung create their collective *shin-myung* and with this, they shatter the forces that desire their death and bring shalom into their lives. This *dae-dong gut* takes place in the *ma-dang* and involves the participation of all of the community. Therefore, this *gut* integrates the site of livelihood with the site of the *gut*. This is the same context that speaks of the fact that minjung art and minjung culture are not removed from the life realities of the minjung. The most important thing, therefore, is that the *gut* reflects the life and realities of the minjung.

As a result, it is appropriate for us to translate the word "spirituality" with the word *shin-myung* or *ki*. *Ki* is used by the Korean people to denote the energy, the spirit, and the vigor of a person that allows the person to act with zeal and pep. I would like to propose that *shin-myung* or *ki* is a better translation than the usual *young-song* (*young* meaning "spirit" and *song* meaning "nature"). But the more important issue is how the Christian community can recreate *gut* and *shin-myung* within the context of its life. The issue confronting us is how we can build a Christian community that is capable of recreating *gut* and *shin-myung*.

This is a difficult task that challenges not only the Korean church but also the theological seminaries, calling for renewal and transformation in their thinking and practice. New insights into the liberating aspects of the *dae-dong gut* and *shin-myung* help us to understand the potential of Korean shamanism for a Korean Christian spirituality that is at once indigenous and liberating. I close with a quotation from Kim Ji Ha:

> Jesus proclaimed the Kingdom of God to the people in the bottom of society. The assemblies of people who surrounded him were revolutionary gatherings because the assembled people, the minjung, are God. Therefore, the proclamation of the Kingdom of God and its Great Opening and Jesus' journeys and the assemblies of minjung who surrounded him were in themselves a *gut*. His being itself was the "Clown" and the "Shaman."

Notes

1. Kim Ji Ha, *Pab* (Rice), a collection of essays in Korean (Waegwan: Benedict Press, 1984). This and subsequent passages are translated from Korean by the author.

4

An Indonesian Contribution
to a Spirituality of Liberation:
Two Perspectives

An Approach from the Javanese World View

A. Nunuk Murniati and I. Kuntara Wiryamartana

The Indonesian people consist of various ethnic groups with a variety of cultural heritages. It is hardly possible to offer a common world view that encompasses all those plural characteristics. As a standpoint for the theological reflection on a "spirituality of liberation," one feature of the Javanese world view will be taken, although in a rather sketchy way. During the course of history, the Javanese world view has absorbed religious values from the great religions, such as Hinduism, Buddhism, and Islam. Nevertheless, it has been able to maintain some basic characteristics which are also shared by other ethnic groups in Indonesia.

Perception of the World, the Human and the Divine

The Javanese world view centers on the universe, the unity and harmony between the "little world" (*jagat cilik* — microcosm) and the "large world" (*jagat gedhe* — macrocosm) with their two dimensions of the "visible" and the "invisible." The life of the human is conceived of in terms of the universe. In the universe everything has its own place, function, and value. In the journey within this phenomenal world, humankind has to know and find its own place, function, and value. To attain this, human beings must scrutinize their own experience of the visible and the invisible, the outer and the inner world. They must move from the outer to the inner world, which is viewed as the genuine reality. This is achieved by "doing" (*laku*), which consists of asceticism (*tapa*) and contemplation or meditation (*samadi*).

In Javanese terms, "God" or the Divine is called by various names, such as "the Creator and Maintainer," "the Maker of Life," and "the Origin/Source and the Goal of Creation." In the deepest inner core of their being, humans can find and meet God as "the Lord of the little world," who is, at the same time, "the Lord of the large world" or God in the cosmic dimension. Although the outer world is easier to grasp because of its visibility and materiality, it is the inner world that is the "genuine reality" in the Javanese world view, for it is through this interior and invisible life that the Divine speaks to the human being.

These two worlds are interrelated and inseparable, so it is the mission of human beings to the outer world as well as to the rest of humankind to strive for the well-being of the whole world. This is not an easy task. In fulfilling this mission, humans need divine guidance to discern the will of the Lord, for the outer world influences and even masks the inner world, often blinding the human heart. Facing the reality of everyday life, human beings need to struggle against the temptations of the outer world, namely, power, position, material possessions, money, inordinate passion, and so forth. Thus, humans experience the possibility of failure and error. Here lies the problem of evil, sin, and suffering.

The Problem of Evil and the Means of Salvation

In Javanese culture, evil is seen as the result of one's own deeds or inherited from one's parents, from which one needs to be purified. The problem of evil is exemplified in the *ruwatan* ceremony, a ritual of purification and liberation that the people (mostly the common people) undergo. The *ruwatan* is carried out in a *wayang* performance, a kind of shadow puppet play, with the *ruwat* ritual as its core and center. The purification is signified by cutting the hair of the person to be purified and pouring water over him or her during the performance.

In the *wayang* repertoire, *Lakon Murwakala* holds a distinctive place as it provides and embodies the mythology of the ritual. This particular puppet play has many versions in Javanese tradition, but it describes why human beings are beset by evil. The story usually centers around the purification of people threatened by evil and serves as meditation during the ritual.

One version features Batara Guru, who lives in the heavens (*kahyangan*) and is the leader of many *bataras* or minor gods. One day Batara Guru, burning with desire, approaches his wife but is refused. This causes his sperm to spill into the ocean below and to flare up violently. Batara Guru asks the help of the other *bataras* to extinguish the flare but none of them succeeds. The flare turns into an embryo and becomes a monster called Batara Kala. This enrages Batara Guru; he turns upon his wife and condemns her to be a demon. Since then, human beings are threatened by evil.

Batara Kala gets hungry and asks his father, Batara Guru, for food. Batara Guru grants his request by setting aside a *wong sukerta* for his meal. *Wong sukerta* means an "unclean person" or "someone threatened by evil." According to the ritual precepts, there are two kinds of *wong sukerta*: persons who are unclean from birth and persons who are unclean through their own misdeeds. (Persons unclean from birth include an only child; one of two children, a boy and a girl, born of the same parents, but without other brothers or sisters; or one of two children, either both boys or both girls, and so on. A person unclean because of his or her own misdeeds is anyone who lets a pot fall when it is on the fire, anyone who breaks a stone rubbing cylinder, and so forth.)

Later on, Batara Guru regrets having granted such food to Batara Kala. He decides to send Batara Wisnu, a minor god, to descend to the world and become a *dhalang*, that is, a *wayang* performer or puppet master. Batara Wisnu has the knowledge of true life and possesses the ability to read the *mantra* or prayer for purification, which is written on Batara Kala's body. Thus, as the *dhalang*, Batara Wisnu can prevent Batara Kala's evil deeds and protect the *wong sukerta*. Batara Wisnu is also known as the "true *dhalang*," or the "*dhalang* sent to proclaim (the Good News)."

The reciting of the *mantra* is the most sacred part of the *ruwat* ritual. After the recitation of the *mantra* at the end of the *wayang* performance, the *dhalang* who plays the part of Batara Wisnu cuts the hair of the persons to be purified and sprinkles or pours water over them. The *wong sukerta* now becomes a "new" person liberated from evil. In some places, the person is given a new name and is called the child of the *dhalang*.

Reflecting upon the *ruwatan* ceremony and its mythology, we find that Batara Kala represents evil, something that threatens the life of humankind and the well-being of the universe. The evil is something "misborn" or "misplaced" in the universe, which in turns engenders "misdeeds" or "evil deeds." Humankind, threatened by evil, becomes liable to "misbirth" or "misdeeds."

In the *ruwat* ritual, human beings are purified or liberated from evil and restored to their true place in the universe. They are given the knowledge of true life to be able to secure their journey within this world. But as they struggle against the difficulties of everyday life, now and then they have to do *laku*, which is both asceticism and contemplation, to care for the world, to deepen their understanding of true reality, and to gain strength and insight from the Divine.

Asceticism and Spirituality

Laku tapa, or asceticism, is an important aspect of Javanese spiritual life. According to ancient Javanese teaching, it is through asceticism that one achieves the aim to bring oneself closer to God. On the one hand, the ancient Javanese practiced asceticism to be one with the whole of nature and feel its goodness, harmony, beauty, and peace. One searches for God through God's creation: the earth, sky, trees, and animals as well as human beings. On the other hand, they practiced asceticism to fight against the worldly temptation to acquire material goods as well as power and prestige, for these are destructive of the inner world, which for them is true reality.

Asceticism need not be practiced in a quiet place; it can be done in a crowded location, even a busy or noisy situation. The interaction between human beings, their interrelationship, work, and activity are all part of asceticism and a means of becoming closer to God. The Javanese like to practice asceticism because they want to become divine. To remain attuned in thought, feeling, and action to other human beings and the rest of creation is precisely to become divine, based on the belief and conviction that all of creation is good.

The reality of the world around us, however, shows disharmony present everywhere. Creation has been misused and abused. The arrogance and avarice of human beings have destroyed peace and harmony. There is malformation in society, with injustice, violence, and disharmony everywhere.

In the Judeo-Christian story of creation, we are told that God saw that all creation is good (Gen. 1:31). Having created man and woman in the divine image and likeness (Gen. 1:27), God then gives them the creation for their life and use. They are given the royal status and responsibility to be stewards of the world and to "command" the cosmos and all in it in a harmonious way. In that way, they are given the grace and blessing to participate in the continuing and never ending work of creation.

But contrary to God's intent, human beings have turned their blessing for harmony into energy for power, manipulation, and domination. Power, wealth, and pleasure have become the objects of idolatrous worship. Human beings are divided into the powerful few (who make the decisions) and the powerless many (who are the victims of decisions). The few dominate the many. This domination is found in the relationship between men and women, women being the victim of male domination. Thus there is disharmony among human beings, and although other forms of domination exist, women remain the double victims.

There is pain, fear, and destruction where there should be harmony, peace, and blessing. Humankind needs salvation from this destructive domination, which can be viewed from two perspectives: the tanathological (personal) and the sociopolitical.

From the tanathological perspective, pain cannot be an excuse for revenge. Pain is not always an enemy to run away from. Javanese culture teaches us that pain is a legitimate school for compassion; it helps us to understand other people in pain. Likewise, pain helps us to understand pleasure and to critique the false, elitist pleasure, which is usually at another's expense. The true pleasures of life are the simple, shareable pleasures. Salvation from domination cannot take the form of running away from pain, but to let pain be pain.

Salvation from domination has a sociopolitical perspective. To work for this salvation is to change the social structures and ideologies that reinforce domination. The world issues are inter-related, with a few people or groups determining the situation and making the decisions, controlled by their system and ide-ology. Salvation entails liberation, a commitment to justice and peace. It must move toward true community building. Women have a special role in this since they form the majority of the victims. Javanese culture must be taken seriously in the search for a spirituality of liberation in Asia.

A Spirituality of Liberation:
An Indonesian Contribution

Josef P. Widyatmadja

The Concretization of Salvation

The Presence of God

The Hebrew phrase *ehye asyer ehye* (Exod. 3:14) can be trans-lated as "I am what I am" (present) or "I will be what I will be" (future). Both are grammatically possible. On the one hand, it intends to convey that God is present and all encompassing. Here the immanent aspect of God is stressed. On the other hand, *ehye asyer ehye* also intends to show that this presence is not static: God's presence is an elusive presence. The "I am" is also "I will be." When we think God is away, God is suddenly present; and when we think God is going to settle down to become our ally, God is suddenly absent, showing God's otherness from us. Thus *ehye asyer ehye* also refers to the transcendent aspect of God.

Talking about God in the framework of God's presence enables us to avoid the antithesis between a "far" and a "near" God or between a God "inside" and a God "outside." To place the immanence and the transcendence of God in an antithetical way distorts the meaning of *ehye asyer ehye*.

The word for "passing by" in Indonesian is *lewat*. Related to this is the word *lawat* (visit). It is used in the Indonesian Bible to translate the Greek word *epeskepsatoo*, as in the phrase "He has visited" in Luke 1:68. A visitor is someone who is "passing by." In English we can say about someone, "Oh, he or she is just passing by," but not in Indonesian. When someone is visiting you (*melawat*), it means he or she is attentive to your needs; he or she wants to help you. The person shows that he or she cares about you. When it is applied to God, we get the picture of a free God who decides freely to be with humankind in order to make every human being free!

God's Visit

Awareness of this elusive but liberating presence comes from within our inner consciousness. Because God is all encompassing, God who dwells in heaven also dwells in the world and in the hearts of humankind. This inner consciousness is not something unconnected with the outside world as has been widely and wrongly believed. It does not necessarily produce an inner-worldly orientation as opposed to an outer-worldly orientation. The inner world is always connected with the outer world through the all-encompassing God. The liberation of the outer world cannot happen in the real sense if there is no awareness of our inner consciousness. In Christ, God has visited the people — God's people, God's world. God makes us free to live in this world, which has been made a place worthy to be lived in through the *ruwat* of Christ.

Ruwat, a Javanese term, means "free from evil" or "liberated from God's punishment." In our Christian terms it is similar to "redemption." Jesus Christ has taken the risk of the cross. He is the ultimate Love who has given up his life for the salvation of the world. Through this kind of *ruwat,* all kinds of evil — either through the faults and sins of humankind or the existential evil that remains a riddle or mystery in God's good creation — have been deabsolutized. Because evil has been deabsolutized, even if it is still real, powerful, and dominant, humankind can be certain of the concreteness of salvation, and all humanity can hope for the future. They can affirm that life is, after all, not a tragedy, and they can and should resist evil, which threatens life.

Contemplation and Struggle

How can we open our inner and outer world to the fact that God has visited God's people through Jesus Christ? By both contemplation and struggle. The word for contemplation in Indonesian and Javanese is *tapa.* By doing *tapa* we become aware that God is continuously visiting the people. This *tapa* does not necessarily demand withdrawal from the world. At most it is a temporary withdrawal, a going back to the source in order to continue the celebration of life. The Javanese even have a phrase for contemplation in the midst of the world — *tapa ngrame.* We do not and cannot contemplate in a vacuum. Our contemplation is complemented by our struggle. We contemplate because we struggle, and we struggle because we contemplate. By contemplation our inner consciousness becomes the dwelling of God and by struggle we accept and celebrate that God has visited this world and made it God's dwelling place. Contemplation and struggle are not means to *imprison* God. As God's presence is an elusive one, God chooses freely to dwell within our hearts and in the world. As Sovereign of the universe, God is greater than our hearts and the world. Jesus is Christ incarnate but also the One who ascends and will come again. Only a free God can make humankind free.

God's Visit to All Creation

We have seen above how God has visited our hearts and the world. It is not just that God has visited the whole of creation. God creates the world and the world is very good. In the creation narrative, the goodness of creation is asserted *before* the creation of humankind (Gen. 1:31). It means that humankind as creation must always regard the other parts of creation as good. Although human beings are referred to as God's image, it does not necessarily mean that humans are above or dominate the other parts of creation. God does not create humankind at the expense of other beings. Created in God's image means to rule in such a way that the goodness of creation can be maintained. The role of the human person is conserving rather than exploiting. The creation is not God. But God visits all of creation. God dwells in creation. It is biblical to say that the creation is praising the Creator (Ps. 19:1–7). This fully conforms with and is affirmed by the beliefs of Asian peoples.

Spirituality of Liberation

The Meaning of Liberation in the Bible
In both the Old Testament and the New Testament, the word "liberation" is similar to the word "salvation." In the Old Testament the word "salvation" is rooted in the word *yeshuah* or "to save." The saving action is done by God. For example, it is written in Genesis 49:18, "I wait for thy salvation, O Lord"; in Exodus 14:13, "You will see the deliverance the Lord will bring you today"; and in Isaiah 12:2, "Behold, God is my salvation." It is clear that from these verses the word *yeshuah* or "to save" points at the action of God and not of human persons. The saving acts can be done toward a person or the people of God as well, but they are always done in the perspective of the history of salvation. In other parts of the Old Testament, the word *moshaoth*, which has a meaning similar to *yeshuah*, namely, "deliverance," is used, as in Psalm 68:20. But it is not used as much as *yeshuah*.

In the New Testament, the word *soteria* is translated as "salvation," as in Luke 1:69, "and has raised up a horn of salvation for us in the house of God's servant, David"; in John 4:22, "We worship what we know, for salvation is from the Jews"; in Acts 13:26, "Brothers and sisters, children of the family of Abraham, and those among you that fear God, to us has been sent the message of this salvation"; and in Romans 1:16, "It is the power of God for salvation to everyone who has faith." The word "salvation" or *soteria* always points at the salvation done by and from God. The meaning of salvation is more often dealing with the salvation of the people rather than of an individual. Salvation refers to God's action not merely for the future, but also at the present time, implemented by God in the history of humankind. The word "liberation" or "freedom" in the Old Testament comes from the word *deror*. For example, in Leviticus 25:10, "and proclaim liberty throughout the land"; and in Isaiah 61:1, "to proclaim liberty to the captives." In Jeremiah 34:16, the word *chophshi* is used for liberation. In the New Testament the word "to liberate" or "to release" is expressed via the word *aphesis*, the same used in Luke 4:18. In the epistles of Paul and Peter, the word *eleutheria* is used for liberation, as in Romans 8:21, "the glorious liberty of the children of God"; in 2 Corinthians 3:17, "where the Spirit of the Lord is, there is freedom"; in 1 Peter 2:16, "Live as free people, yet without using your freedom as a pretext for evil."

By exploring these data, it is clear that the words "salvation" and "liberation" are always related to the saving or liberating acts of God toward humankind. Salvation or liberation always refers to actual situations and to the hope of God's people. Praises and songs of God's salvation are usually referred to the salvation expected by the people of God as a whole.

The Meaning of Spirituality of Liberation

What is the meaning of the word "spirituality" for us? The word "spirituality" often points to human feelings and inner life. Paul Tillich explains spirituality as "the feelings, acts, and experiences of individuals or groups in their solitude." It has to do with activities of human self-transcendence as they are related to the holy, to a deity, to a sacred cosmos or to an ultimate concern. At a glance, spirituality seems to be merely concerned with religion that has nothing to do with a person's daily life. Spirituality is often used to refer to the human person's pursuit of holiness, personal salvation, or higher level of devotion.

But spirituality does not belong to the religious sphere only. Spirituality is a consciousness or attitude that evolves within an individual or community. Spirituality is both a consciousness and a means of achieving the goal or final hope of a person or a group. The consciousness and means of reaching the vision of

God's people is precisely Christian spirituality. In the World Council of Churches' (WCC) assembly in Nairobi in 1975, M. M. Thomas stated: "Perhaps what Christians are particularly called to work out is what might be called a 'spirituality for combat.' Can our struggle become part of our celebration of God as we understand Him [sic]? How might we help each other to conduct our struggle that they become part of our worship?"

The contribution of holiness in action, combining struggle with contemplation, has been remarkable. M. M. Thomas himself gives this warning: "Let us not forget that our struggle is not merely against others but also against ourselves, not against flesh and blood, but against false spirituality of the idolatry of race, nation and class and of the self-righteousness of ideals which reinforce collective structures of inhumanity and oppression."

The main thought of M. M. Thomas's "spirituality for combat" was put into questions by the Urban Rural Mission of the Christian Conference of Asia (URM-CCA) in Sri Lanka in 1982. Is there really any spirituality for combat? For the URM personnel with experiences of struggling with the people, spirituality should arise from "combat" or struggle with the people for social justice. Is there any spirituality that can be given to "combat" or "liberation"? Without incarnation in the midst of the people's struggle, it will be impossible for a person or a group to have the experience or possess a spirituality of liberation.

Gustavo Gutiérrez put "conversion" as an important part of spirituality. "Conversion means a radical transformation of ourselves, it means thinking, feeling, and living as Christ present in exploited and alienated man [sic]." However, Yap Kim Hao, former CCA General Secretary, prefers to use the word "repentance" in relation to spirituality. In Asia, the word "conversion" too often gives the image of people becoming Christians in a process of "Christianization," so that the main purpose is not liberation of the people, but "Christianization." "Repentance" can give a better sense of returning to Jesus and the Reign of God.

Experience in the Field

Spirituality of liberation is not the monopoly of the churches or religious groups, but rather it belongs to anyone who longs for justice, peace, and the integrity of creation. We often consider Javanese farmers to be people who depend too much on fate, who show a lack of the spirit to struggle, and who are unaware of their rights and responsibilities. In past history, their struggles for justice all ended in tragic failure, because they did not have any ideology, or charismatic leader, or any organization and technology. But this did not happen to the farmers in their recent struggle against the government's acquisition of their lands for a big dam construction. The farmers demanded that their lands be exchanged with lands near their village. They refused to transmigrate out of Java island, or to accept inadequate payment or infertile land in the region. In order to pressure the farmers, the government intimidated and arrested them, charging them as members of banned organizations after unlawfully altering their citizen cards. In addition, the government issued unjust decrees about land payments, and even went as far as inundating their villages.

For more than three years, the people suffered from intimidation and pressure, but they organized themselves to resist and avoid any physical violence. The attitude of Jesus and Gandhi (*ahimsa* or nonviolence) was carried out by them in their struggle for their rights. Sympathy and solidarity were expressed by university students and staff, the press, spiritual leaders, nongovernmental organizations, and so on. In April 1989, the government finally agreed to fulfill the farmers' demands by exchanging their land with land of the same quality around the dam, giving them the right to cultivate the land for agriculture, and compensating for damaged property such as crops and houses. The government also agreed to give the farmers new citizen cards, to confirm their local organizations, and to provide them with clean water facilities, a health center, irrigation, a school, and a village meeting hall, among other things.

One of the reasons the people could persevere and succeed in their struggle was the spiritual relationship between them and their land. Furthermore, they made use of their own local organization in order to resist the unjust demands being made on them. They did not resort to violence, and thus made it difficult for the government to charge them as common criminals.

When their village was inundated by the government, the

farmers understood it as a fulfillment of one of their ancestors' legends. Based on this well-known legend, the people were not to leave their area because the abundant period will take place when "fish consume the coconut flower" (*wader mangan manggar*). This meant that when the coconut palm trees are covered with water, then the fish can consume their flowers. This could not possibly happen under normal conditions because the flowers are very high in the coconut palm tree. Moreover, the people interpreted the legend of "fish consume the coconut flower" as a story of people from the lower stratum defeating the strong and powerful officials in the struggle for justice.

The attitude of resistance (spirituality of resistance) and the holding fast to the legend that has become an ideology were important factors in the people's struggle. The legend inherited from their ancestors had become the power of their struggle that reinforced their attitude not to give in to any kind of pressure or cruel actions. The case of the farmers' struggle showed an example of their spirituality of liberation. The spirituality of the farmers came from their experience, culture, challenges, and hopes. The spirituality was not individual or mystical, but a historical struggle. The struggle of the farmers created changes in developmental moral values nationally and internationally. The statement that development demands victims or sacrifices from lowly and weak people was rejected. The price of development actually must be paid by the *whole* people, especially the rich and powerful, who should naturally pay more.

A Christian spirituality of liberation should not be separated from the spirituality of liberation of Asian peoples. To become a Christian does not mean to be separated from the community of common people. Christian spirituality is not against the spirituality of liberation that has already existed within our legends or cultures. On the contrary, Christian spirituality should be capable of providing answers, directions, and meanings for the spirituality already possessed by the people. In other words, it should become a dynamic factor within the existing spirituality of the people. Introducing Christian spirituality is not identical with introducing Christian rituality (worship). The practice of Christian ritual is not the same as Christian spirituality. Our problem remains how to actualize the Christian spirituality of liberation in the midst of Asian cultures and religions.

A Spirituality of Liberation in Asia

In general, the people of Asia are farmers. They are commonly considered as having no initiative, as obedient people who depend on fate. They do not have property or the technology to protest against the exploitation and extortion practiced in the feudal or capitalist system. Farmers in Asia are the victims of development. Indeed, they do not have the power, property, or proper technology to face exploitation. But they still have a spirituality of resistance or liberation. Their expressions of protest against the exploitative community system are often not so extraordinary. This leads to the impression that Asian farmers are too dependent on fate. Actually their hopes and dreams are very much alive, but they express them through their culture and way of life, so the expressions of their protest differ from those of farmers in other places.

An illustration that shows the spirituality of liberation in Asia is a conversation among a coconut tree, a clove tree, a banyan tree, and grass. Each of them tries to show superiority and strength. The coconut tree says to the other trees, "I am a tree that knows everything. I am tall and my eyes can see in all directions without any obstruction. I am the most useful tree for people, because all parts of me can be used for their needs. My trunk, leaves, and fruit are all useful." Seeing the coconut tree's pride, the clove tree says, "I am the most liked by farmers, because the clove fruits I produce can provide them with property. All farmers are mad about cloves because they can get rich." Then the banyan tree also boasts of its superiority and says, "I am the most powerful tree. People from the lowest class up to the highest officials come every Thursday to worship me and make offerings of flowers and benzoins. They come to ask for property, jobs, partners, and power, and I can give them all of these. Therefore they always worship me, for if they do not, I will not give them power or position."

After boasting of their respective superiorities, the three trees ask the grass under their feet what it possesses. With a low voice the grass says to the three trees, "My fate is the worst among all plants. I am considered low and useless. When I grow higher they cut me, so again I am short. Animals like horses, sheep, and cattle come and trample on me while grazing. Afterwards they defecate on me so that every part of my body becomes smelly for anyone who passes near me." For the grass, there is nothing to be proud of. It cannot compete with the high technology of the coconut palm tree or with the wealth of the clove tree. Neither has it the power to stand against the banyan tree.

The condition of the grass is similar to that of the common people who have nothing to be considered by other trees. It is impossible for the common people to compete with the intellectual strength of scholars (coconut palm tree), or the economic power of the affluent (clove tree), or the existing political power (banyan tree). These "trees" often look down on the "grass."

But the poor condition of the grass does not automatically mean that it is weaker than the coconut palm or the clove tree or the banyan. When the storm and the heavy rains come, the tall coconut palm, the lush clove tree, and the big banyan tree cannot stand against the wind and flood. They all collapse and are destroyed. But the lowly grass survives through all kinds of weather. The heat of the sun or the flood cannot carry the grass away and ruin it. It stands while other trees collapse.

This is what we want to note about the spirituality of resistance of Asian peoples. The spirituality of liberation in Indonesia, for example, is expressed as the spirituality of resistance. We prefer the word "resist" to "combat." The protest of the grass (lower stratum people) against cruel actions is demonstrated in resistance in order to stay alive under any condition. But the hope for change and transformation never dies. It is only the grass (or common people) that can grow steadily when change or transformation happens. The hope of transformation is believed to be a hope that will surely be fulfilled.

A spirituality of liberation cannot be equated with a spirituality of revenge. Revenge can never result in genuine liberation; it will create anarchy instead. Rather, it is with a spirituality of compassion that a spirituality of liberation can be identified. The two cannot be separated. Without compassion there can never be true liberation. It is also true that without liberation, compassion is nonsense, for compassion does not mean simply accepting fate without protest or any interest in transformation. Thus Christian spirituality cannot be one of revenge or violence, but rather one that tends toward liberation and compassion.

The Nature of Our Mission

Being a Christian does not merely mean being a worshiper of Christ. Neither does one become the owner of Christ or the only special one who belongs to Christ. The value of being a follower of Christ is following what was done by Jesus Christ as both divine and human. A true Christian, a true follower of Christ, does and acts as Jesus did in his life rather than speaks or preaches about Jesus.

What did Jesus do? How did he act? He preached the Kingdom of God; he preached a new heaven and a new earth. "The blind receive their sight and the lame walk, lepers are cleansed and the deaf hear, the dead are raised up, and the poor have good news preached to them" (Matt. 11:5). Jesus released human dignity from all kinds of bondage to reveal the *imago Dei*. Even a prostitute repented and changed her mind, testifying to the good news (John 4:1–30). If Jesus said that his food is to do the will of the One who sent Him, then all his disciples, all his followers, have to be conscious that following Christ means to do the will of God. Let every single human live humanly. The grace, the mercy, the love, and the justice of God ought to be manifested in all aspects of life. That is primary and basic. The poor are not only the materially poor, but all who have been bereft of human dignity, all those whose *imago Dei* cannot shine through because of so many kinds of bondage.

Nowadays we face a variety of missionary options. What kind of mission will the church or the Christian have? In our Indonesian context, transforming society so that there will no longer be any poor is uppermost. The number of poor is increasing, their faces scattered amidst laborers, peasants, fisherfolk, political prisoners — impoverished, discriminated against, oppressed, and exploited. They are powerless and marginalized, and deemed as second class in the society. Will the church be able to practice holistic ministry without trying to transform society to benefit the poor? Whatever values the church has, if these do not demonstrate concern for the poor, who are oppressed and marginalized, then these values are worthless indeed. The preferential option for the poor is ultimately to serve and strengthen all. To proclaim the gospel is to bring not only the poor to "look forward to a new heaven and a new earth," but all of us "living in the Kingdom of God."

The presence of God and God's work amidst human beings has to be compassionate by nature, so that involvement with the oppressed and marginalized in order to resist injustice is a primary and basic act of compassion in God's world. Poverty is a concrete form of bondage, and it is the role of Christians to be engaged in the liberation of all human beings from it. A protest against poverty is a form of solidarity with the poor, and it is Christian.

The challenge of the churches or of Christians in the present situation is within their own selves — not just how to defend the ignored or the defenseless people who are treated unjustly, but to eradicate the doubt and fear of defending and helping the discriminated person or people. It is commitment to the poor and the oppressed, so that "the word became flesh and dwelt among us, full of grace and truth" (John 1:14) can be preached not just as words but as something that really happens through all human beings. Most of the Christians in Indonesia (and Asia), *de facto*, cannot be included among the poor; most of the churches and the Christians are aligned with the power of affluence. How then to preach the presence of God, that God dwells among us?

The poor ought to be conscious that they are fully human beings, that they exist as creatures with dignity, that all of God's creation is for the benefit of all God's children, including the poor. They must have a self-awareness that they are created in the image of God. As Christians, we love to be called children of God; however, we cannot claim to be the children of God without helping others to become who God meant them to be. God wants all to be God's children, all human beings to live in the Kingdom of God (1 Tim. 2:3–4).

Revealing human dignity is a gospel mandate. To be compassionate is a gospel mandate; it is not an arbitrary choice. One cannot be committed to the gospel unless one is involved in struggling against poverty; it is radical obedience to God. One cannot obey God without being involved. To protest against poverty is to eradicate acquisitiveness or avarice. Solidarity with the poor does not mean shunning the wealthy and their affluence; it means warning them that wealth and affluence ought to be shared (1 Tim. 6:17–19).

Praying and praxis, contemplation and action are inseparable. Can we be a praying church if we are not also going to be a church that attempts to put the meaning of those prayers into praxis? Contemplation is the deepest awareness of the human existence before God. The church reflects whether the church's faith is a living faith or not. Insofar as that faith is put to work, it makes us not only transformed agents, but also agents for transformation. We cannot be an agent for transformation unless we ourselves are going to be more transformed into the image of God who is always involved in the business of liberating.

This task is not easy. The churches in Indonesia have a Western/European face that came together with colonialism, and, as such, became alienated from the people. This historical heritage has a lot of influence on the churches today in aligning themselves with the wealthy or powerful. They are unwilling to leave the comfort they have in order to follow the steps of Jesus of Nazareth. Even the church tends to be selfish, focusing on her own internal problems and not caring for her neighbors. The church has to be bold to look at herself and her life, and to contemplate her task. Called by the Spirit to live a simple lifestyle, she must be prepared to be changed and to change.

Interfaith Relationships within a Spirituality of Liberation

It is well known that Vatican Council II and the World Council of Churches have fostered positive attitudes toward the other religions and faiths. We can trace the development of thought within the WCC.

In the General Assembly at Evanston (1954) the revival of non-Christian religions and new ideologies obliged the churches to take new directions in fulfilling their missionary mandate. In 1956 the Central Committee decided to launch the study on the

Word of God and the living faiths. From this study appeared a shift of trend. The missionary trend gave way to the trend of living together with people of different faiths. In 1960 Hendrik Kraemer published his study on world cultures and world religions. He tried to show the exclusiveness of the Christian religion.

The main criticism of this study came from Paul Devanandan, who stated that, rather than sharpening the exclusive factors, Christians should strive for possibilities of living together with people of other faiths and contribute to the development of emerging nations in which people of many religions and faiths live together. Beginning from the 1960s, all the meetings and conferences have tended to stress "dialogue" and "encounter." The reason is partly because a growing number of the members of the WCC are churches from the Third World where Christianity as a minority lives among the majority of other living religions.

In the Nairobi Assembly (1975), a more or less balanced view was agreed upon. On the one hand, Christians should strive for "dialogue in community" with people of other faiths; but on the other hand, the uniqueness of Christ and the mandate of proclamation were also stressed. Dialogue cannot prosper in a real sense if we try to ignore the uniqueness of each religion's experience and tradition.

In general, the tendency is to move away from looking at people of other religions as objects of evangelization "to the view that they are our neighbors." In Indonesia, the term *sesama manusia*, the same human being as oneself, is used. The Asian theologian Choan-Seng Song has proposed to use the term "decisiveness" of Christ rather than the usual word "exclusiveness." We do not deny Christ when we try to meet others in an encounter, but on the other hand we do not claim him as exclusively ours. We have to move beyond dogmatism and syncretism toward a genuine spirituality that fosters genuine encounters with people from other religions.

Speaking of the relationship between Christians and Muslims, the Vatican Council II reminds us:

Over the centuries many quarrels and dissensions have arisen between Christians and Muslims. The sacred Council now pleads with all to forget the past, and urges that a sincere effort be made to achieve mutual understanding; for the benefit of all men and women, let them together preserve and promote peace, liberty, social justice and moral values. (*Nostra Aetate*, 3)

Together with all people of good will the church is called to struggle for peace, liberty, social justice, and moral values. In other words, different religions and faiths enter into a common spirituality of liberation.

We stand as Christians, holding Jesus Christ as the dynamic criterion of our faith. We are not honest to ourselves and to others if we abandon this assumption. This Jesus Christ cannot be absorbed totally by any faith or religion. No faith or religion can claim that it contains Christ totally. Openness is a necessity for the dynamic following of Christ. As Francis J. Moloney has said (*Pacifica* 1, [1988]:42):

Who Jesus Christ is, and what he asks for from all who claim to be responding to his call to "follow" (Mark 1:16–20) cannot be "controlled" or "contained" by *any* religion, *any* culture or *any* history. The life and teaching, death and resurrection of Jesus of Nazareth stand as a challenge to the absolutisation of any particular culture, religion or history.

The expressions of Christian religion, whether in the forms of doctrines, worship, or the whole structure with its leadership, are also limited. Therefore, self-criticism of religion is necessary. The churches are helped by other faiths, religions, and different cultures to understand and to live out better the gospel and the mystery of Christ. Hence, we can speak here about dialogue as openness to God and mutual evangelization. From this point of view we can take a step to understand the dialogue of life. Our starting point is Christian faith. This faith urges us to live out the gospel concretely in a common social experience, common suffering, and common struggle of liberation. A common struggle of liberation with brothers and sisters of other religions and faith is not a tactic to Christianize, but a demand of our faith, a demand of faithfulness to Christ.

5

An Indian Search for a Spirituality
of Liberation

Indian Preparatory Group[1]

Introduction

The search for a spirituality of liberation is part of an ongoing concern of EATWOT (Ecumenical Association of Third World Theologians) and other groups who are committed to evolving a theology that is integral to the struggles of the poor in the Third World. It is often pointed out that poverty and religiousness are the two dominant characteristics of the Asian reality, and the interrelationship between these should receive serious attention in our liberation movements and in theological reflection in Asia. Visible structures of religion — its rituals and institutions — and the spirituality or spiritualities that are embedded in them exercise a powerful influence over the poor in Asia. How far is this influence oppressive or liberative? This is a question that is constantly being raised.

In India, with its rich heritage of religion and culture, there is a bewildering variety of spiritualities. What role do they play in the movements for liberation? What forms of spirituality have been and continue to be used to legitimize the dominance of upper castes or classes over the masses? Is there a spirituality that is germane to the life and experience of the poor in our villages and slums? Are there new forms of spirituality that are emerging out of people's movements? In short, in what sense can we speak of a spirituality of liberation in the Indian context?

This and other related questions were the basis of a consultation organized by the Indian regional committee of EATWOT from February 27–March 2, 1989, in Madras. About sixteen participants from all over India attended. Presentations were made on the following issues: an Indian search for a spirituality of liberation; tribal identity—a liberation potential; Islamic struggles for minority rights; the *dalit* context for a spirituality of liberation; an understanding of Tukaram as a liberation poet; the spirituality of women's struggles for liberation; and the liberation motif in the People's Union for Civil Liberties—a human rights experience.

The following statement incorporates the main findings of the consultation.

The Indian Context

We meet at a time when the victims of the Bhopal Gas Disaster of 1984 are demonstrating in front of the Supreme Court in Delhi against the Indian government's total sell-out to the Union Carbide company of the United States. (The Indian government has agreed to a settlement of a paltry U. S. $470 million from Union Carbide and has failed to set a code of ethics and safety measures for multinational investment in India.) It is estimated that more than twenty thousand people died and many thousands more were maimed for life when the deadly MIC gas leaked out of the factory and snuffed life out of Bhopal in December 1984. Bhopal is a grim reminder of the devastating effects of a Eurocentric industrial model of development that has become the model for the world. It is a model of development which is capitalist in orientation, built on the maximization of profits and the compulsions of market forces. This development model is built on the depredation of the earth and its resources.

The imposition of this model of development and two hundred years of British colonial rule in India have led to the destruction of traditional economies, the people's arts and crafts, and their way of life and livelihood. Capitalist forces have been unleashed, initiating a process by which the country's internal resources have been made subservient to the industrial expansionist interests of the West. This model of development is built on a social structure, the main bulwark of which is caste feudalism. Forty-odd years of independence from British rule have only witnessed further pauperization of the people. The numbers below the poverty line are increasing by leaps and bounds, and every year we hear reports of men, women, and children dying of starvation. In the face of this horrific specter of starvation, we continue to spend our scarce resources on missile testing ranges, big dams, and nuclear plants. The people who are largely the victims of this development model are displaced *dalits* and tribals. The imposition of the Westminster model of parliamentary democracy has failed to take into account the cultural and ethnic diversities of our country, and this has resulted in the lack of political power and representation for the various oppressed identities. Even the education system continues to keep our people enslaved and divided, perpetuating the interests of the ruling elite. Christians have played a role in promoting this kind of an education, sometimes unconsciously, as they merely continued what the missionary enterprise had set in motion for the colonial rulers.

While the model of development opted for has led to this rapid pauperization, thereby increasing unemployment and alienation from the land for the toiling millions, it necessarily follows that, at the same time, a small handful enjoy grotesque levels of wealth. An inevitable component of this development model is the subjugation of India to global economic powers, heavy dependence for aid and investment, and the tightening noose of external debt. This has led to the country's entanglement in the global economic network, a disastrous consequence of which is the rapid militarization and nuclearization of Indian society. The last two decades have also seen India emerge as a big power in the region with expansionist ambitions.

The development model has led to the undermining of the experiences and creativity of various oppressed identities, such as *dalits*, tribals, minorities, smaller nationalities, and women. The main burden of the continuing economic crisis falls on these sections. Whenever these groups have attempted to rise and claim their legitimate rights and have struggled to preserve their identities, they have been crushed by a ruthlessly armed state. The state continuously acquires a battery of special powers, anti-people laws, and military strength to crush the people's aspirations and struggles. An ugly fascism masquerading as "the Indian nationalism" has now been let loose on the land, and it constitutes a threat to the richness of Indian civilization with its mosaic of cultures and peoples.

Unfortunately an ideology of Hindu nationhood and Brahmanic culture, as the norm, is a weapon in the hands of the state, which in turn engenders a dangerous insularity and exclusivism among the minorities. A vision of nation building has been propagated that attempts to subsume all identities other than that of a narrow ruling stratum. This stratum consists of a small coterie of privileged castes and classes. In this situation we view the assertion of diversity and plurality as attempts to strengthen the great composite Indian civilization.

The Culture of Resistance

But then the culture of resistance to the forces of death has constantly reasserted its power as people's movements have emerged and grown in independent India. Workers' and peasants' movements have formed the bulwark of demands for transformation of society, and these have been supported and buttressed by newly emerging movements of *dalits*, tribals, and women. The organized power of human rights and civil liberties groups and environmental and peace movements are also forces to be reckoned with. The newly emerging voices of protest and rage are rooted in the discovery of new paradigms of analysis and action, as the search for a new India and a new world gains momentum. Here we describe briefly just three of these movements and the spiritual dimensions they provide.

Dalit *Movement*

Fifteen percent of the Indian population are *dalits*. This new name for the oppressed people of this land represents the aspirations of those who had been viewed as "outcastes" in the caste hierarchy. The *dalit* movement has reasserted the dignity of millions of people who had been crushed to dust by the Aryan/

Brahmanic Hinduism. *Dalit* women have been described as the "dust of the dust," thrice oppressed and therefore clearly the least of the "little ones" in Indian society. The nature of the emerging *dalit* consciousness — ideas, feelings, experience, performance — is vital in understanding how *dalits* envisage their future and the common future of this country. *Dalits* are now aware that historically they are the indigenous people of India forming one community with the tribals. Over the centuries they not only lost their territory, but were also scattered across the land, enslaved by the Brahmin priests and ruling classes, and made into outcastes in a system of institutionalized inequality — i.e., the caste system — which is a product of Brahmin civilization.

The building up of the *dalit* future identity involves the task of rediscovering and reconstructing its past history and heritage, as no identity can be built in a cultural and historical vacuum. This process of reconstruction has to begin from the known Indus civilization in India and its ancient roots. The history of conflict, alienation, and cultural subjugation of *dalits* by the dominant culture and its agents, is told in the language of myths, stories, hybrid religious symbols, and rituals. We have also archeological and linguistic data available to reconstruct the outlines and in some cases the details of subjugation.

This process of the *dalits* regaining a new identity essentially is in conflict not only with material interests of the ruling caste groups but also with their cultural and religious hegemony. Therefore what is required is a spirituality that endures conflict and provides hope for the new. In Christian symbolism can this be the spirituality of the cross?

The practitioners of this spirituality are small groups and organizations made up of *dalits* and others who have taken upon themselves the task of redeeming *dalit* human dignity and their conviction that they would humanize their opponents in the process.

These groups draw on the resources of all spiritual traditions to sustain themselves, as in the case of Swami Anand Thirth who remembered Jesus' words, "If someone slaps you on the right cheek, then offer him your left," when he was beaten up by caste Hindus for taking *dalit* children to a marketplace. At the same time, Swami Anand Thirth found it impossible to belong to any one of the established religions with their dogmas and priests, as he believed that all religions are controlled as social institutions by the dominant caste or class groups. *Dalit* youth in today's movement emboldened by the Siddhar/Cittar saints and prophets[2] who had denounced the scriptures and *Vedas* of established religion, draw on the symbols of ordinary folk religiosity.

In short, to experience the cruelty of the untouchability and poverty of the *dalits*, one needs to identify with their lot in life. But there is also a spirituality of association with the cause of the *dalits* possible for members of all religious communities. This consists in creating a religious consciousness among the masses, which shows understanding toward *dalit* issues and problems. Historians, social scientists, and theologians can practice this spirituality by understanding their disciplines from the perspective of the *dalits*. Indian theology will have to break new ground and transform itself into a theology of liberation. It has to become a theology from the underside of history informed by the perspectives of *dalits*, tribals, women, and creation.

Women's Movement

The present phase of the women's movement in India can be traced to the early 1970s when a fourteen-year-old girl, Mathura, was raped in a police station in Maharashtra, and the Supreme Court rescinded a Maharashtra High Court decision indicting the two guilty policemen. Women took this as an opportune moment to organize to challenge the more than a century-old unjust rape law and the violence against women that society seems to legitimize. What began as basically a middle-class urban movement focusing on what can be narrowly defined as "women's issues" spread within a decade to the rural areas, and now it is in fact rural women who form the backbone of the movement. Women, by their participation in the autonomous women's movement and in the struggles of the people, have begun formulating new feminist questions and paradigms of involvement for the total transformation of Indian society. Several issues have emerged out of this quest.

Feminist critical involvement in liberation. The deepening economic crisis, the increasing destabilization of the government, the growing use of army, police, and paramilitary forces, and the lopsided "development" model all seriously affect women's lives. Low legal status, economic and political marginalization, and cultural and religious pressures erode women's self-esteem. The assertiveness of fundamentalist and communalist forces constitutes an additional threat to women's independence and participation. Caste hierarchy and stratification and the dalitness of *dalit* women make them particular targets for patriarchal violence and control.

Women have challenged the Eurocentric-androcentric science- and technology-oriented model of development opted for by the planners, which is based on the "mastery" of creation and on the undermining of the experiences of those on the fringes of society—women, *dalits*, and tribals particularly. Women's groups have struggled against the use of medical and genetic technologies that abuse women's bodies and reproductive gifts. They have also supported tribals and others in their struggle against big dams or nuclear plants. They have supported the *dalit* movement in its search for dignity and selfhood. They have also challenged traditionally accepted political paradigms that have not taken cultural questions of caste, religion, tribal identity, and patriarchy as seriously as they should in analysis and in strategies for action.

The feminist liberation paradigm offers to the peoples' movements a critique in terms of leadership, decision-making processes, their hierarchy of patriarchal relationships, and also their very "masculine" methodologies and strategies. Thus the feminist paradigm calls for a critical involvement in liberation struggles.

Celebration of plurality. If we understand theological or spiritual activity in an academic sense as reflections on or interpretations of scriptures, then women participating in such activity will be a minuscule minority in India. However, women in the secular movement easily transcend narrow divisions of faith, caste, and ideology and come together to reflect and act on issues of national importance.

While questions of female survival do tend to absorb the greatest attention in the women's movement, there is recognized a need to reappropriate religion from right-wing, fundamentalist groups and to discover liberation strands in all religions. And this is in spite of the fact that the patriarchalization of all religions has led to the diminishing of the status and dignity of women.

Any theological activity cannot be done, therefore, in isolation from this attempt to express the celebration of solidarity in pluralism that is the overarching characteristic of the women's movement in India. Feminist theology in India, therefore, seeks to reappropriate and reinterpret the Bible from the perspective of women in struggle, and to give new meaning and courage to women in the midst of their violence-filled lives. A critique of traditional, patriarchal images of God and of Christology and a search for new, more liberative, compassionate, healing, and nurturing images assume significance.

Popular religiousness. Recently feminists have shown an interest in exploring popular religiousness, precisely because it is a religion of the marginalized, and often it contains elements of protest that can be reenergized to become a force for social change. Feminist theologians have discovered a special significance in this because in many of the popular religious experiences women have played an important role and they are in essence women's liberation-centered—though of course these experiences too have been distorted by patriarchal onslaughts.

Feminist spirituality. The life experiences of all the women who find new power in the autonomous women's movement are, indeed, essentially a spirituality. Women's attempts to break through the culture of silence and to transform their pain into political power are a deeply spiritual experience. The attempts to draw on creative expressions—dance, drama, poetry, music, art, story-telling, and folklore—to give expression to the new-found consciousness and energy is spirituality. The longing to reclaim their femininity, as they would define it, and to reclaim their right to control their own reproductive capabilities is spirituality.

It is a spirituality that would say "yes" to life and "no" to forces of death. It is a life-affirming, nurturing, creating spirituality. In the shedding of blood, the cleansing and preparing for new life month after month, women have drawn new power that will no longer control and stifle their creativity, but will be symbolic of the longing for a new and transformed India. In sisterhood, in communal selfhood, in solidarity with all other oppressed people, in the simplicity of the lifestyle of the movement, and in their commitment to healing a wounded creation and wounded world, women are expressing a new spirituality.

Tribal Liberation Movements

There are about 75 million tribal people in our country (out of 225 million outcastes; out of 700 million Indians) spread from the northeast region through the Jharkhand region and over Madhya Pradesh, Gujarat, Rajasthan, and Maharashtra, and down to South Orissa and North Andhra to Karnataka, Tamilnadu, and Kerala.

The industrial model of development, which was introduced into all parts of the country by the Indian government, with its emphasis on individualism and profit, came as a cultural shock to the socioeconomic, cultural, and political structure of tribal societies. The already continuing struggles of the tribals against the onslaughts of the dominant Hindu society were aggravated by this development model that eroded the traditional way of life and livelihood of tribals, alienating them from the land and from creation, and leading to their rapid pauperization.

History is replete with expressions of rebellion from tribal populations, of which the Santal rebellion in 1851–52 in the last century is the best known. When India became independent, the tribals had great hopes of just and fair dealings from their Indian brothers and sisters. But this trust and hope was soon dashed to the ground, and the tribals found their situation deteriorating even further. The five-year plans and their industrially oriented focus has deeply affected tribal life. Almost all big dams, factories, hydroelectric and nuclear plants, and missile testing ranges are constructed on tribal homelands, with scant regard for tribal life and culture. To the tribals the colonizing of their lands is a continuing characteristic of the so-called "development" efforts of the dominant groups.

This century has also witnessed some strong liberation movements for tribal identity. The most important are the liberation movements in northeast India for political autonomy, the demand for a Gondwanaland in Madhya Pradesh, and the

Jharkhand movement in north central India, in south Bihar, West Bengal, northern Orissa, and eastern Madhya Pradesh.

The Jharkhand movement has emerged as the major tribal liberation movement in our history. The demand for a separate Jharkhand will cover a population of about 30 million people, of which two-thirds will be tribals. The history of this movement can be traced to 1926, when a few young tribal Christians came together to reflect on the plight of their people. By 1939 the movement grew to become the Adhibhasi Mahasabha (Tribal Organization) under the leadership of an Oxford graduate, Jaipal Singh. In 1952 the people's movement became a political party, and the Jharkhand Party and the political demand for a separate state took shape. In the years from 1952 to 1957 the Jharkhand Party became the opposition group in the Bihar Assembly and could ensure the intensification of reservations for tribals in education and employment. With the reorganization of Indian states in 1956, the demand for a separate Jharkhand state for the tribals was rejected, and they were divided and got scattered to four states—most of them in Bihar, but some in Madhya Pradesh, Orissa, and West Bengal. This was a setback to the movement and the stability of the party. The political situation in the nation at large, and the one-party hegemony at the center and in most of the states, added to the undermining of the Jharkhand movement. The tribals felt betrayed by their leaders and the movement weakened. But the tribal spirit for liberation was never completely destroyed.

The 1970s gave a new impetus to the Jharkhand movement with the reassertion of the language and culture of tribals by middle-class intellectuals. By 1977 the movement took on a militant posture. The demand for tribal identity was massively revived in the consciousness of the people through songs, stories, dramas, and so forth. The recent formation of the Coordination Committee, which brings together all the liberation efforts into one combined fold, is another hopeful step forward. With this it has become more inclusive of all oppressed groups in the region, such as the Sadans, who are Muslims.

The long history of struggles, protests, action, and reflection has taught the tribals valuable lessons. The Jharkhand movement has now become a movement of reconciliation between the tribals and other marginalized groups in that region. In this process it has become conscious of the importance of including dimensions of national and human liberation. It is a liberation movement of the deep human spirit enshrined primarily in the tribal vision of life and experience. This tribal ethos has to be restored in the movement and in the people, as it has become watered down through pressures from dominant ideologies. Its most basic component is the sustaining of the continuum of the relationship among nature, humanity, and spirit, which is the vital criterion for humanity's desire to be human. The egalitarian society that is basic to tribal culture has to be revitalized and promoted in this process. Community ownership of the means of production, and the use of the produce for the good of all, are tribal values that need to be implemented once again. The tribal concept of equal participation of all in social and political decision making, with stress on consensus, needs to be revived and used in the Jharkhandi socioeconomic, cultural, and political life. All this implies that the demand for the creation of a Jharkhand state within the Indian nation is a vision of a unique and new form of government. The tribals believe that the establishment of the Jharkhand state is a means of restoring tribal and human values, residues of which can still be found in tribal societies in spite of the onslaughts of the majority community.

The struggle for liberation in Jharkhand continues today, with much pain, as tribals contend against the police and military power of the dominant group. It is a countercultural movement challenging the "modern," scientific, and technological view of life. The Jharkhandi liberation movement envisions an alternative to the presently existing lifestyle of our nation. When the dream of a Jharkhand state becomes a reality, then it will be able to experiment with this new vision, undergirded by tribal historical and traditional value systems. This search is indeed an expression of the deep spirituality of tribal societies. The institutionalized church is not able to respond in the same way.

Toward a New Spirituality

Of such movements and struggles, of such visions and dreams, spirituality is a constitutive factor. Spirituality is intrinsic to action for liberation. All women and men in our country or elsewhere who have striven and continue to strive against exploitation and oppression and for justice and dignity for all are spiritual women and men. Their stories must be told, their memory cherished, and their inspiration carried forward.

The spiritual is not a dimension added to the people's struggles and protests in order to provide motivation and sacrality. When we stand for justice and freedom and for people's right to life with dignity, we stand for those realities and values in terms of which all faiths image the Mystery of the Divine. That is why, for Jeremiah, to do justice is to "know" God. When we stand with the oppressed, we stand with the one who always takes their side and acts for their liberation (Ps. 103:6). The downtrodden people with their history of hope and struggle are the locus, the place, of authentic encounter with God. In confronting injustice and working for a new India, a new world, where people are equal and free, and where resources are for all, there exists a profound spirituality even if it is not recognized, made explicit, or named. In the New Testament story of the good Samaritan, a non-religious person's "secular" action (as distinct from religious or priestly behavior) is commended as belonging within the realm and purposes of God (Luke 10:29–37).

In the parable of the last judgment, Jesus interprets the unnamed depths, the "Beyond," the transcendent dimensions of deeds of justice and compassion done by people who had never named any faith. Having faith and belonging in the Realm of God consists not in recital of creeds but in the doing of God's will for this earth, on this earth. Spirituality is the people's experience that their struggle is not meaningless, that life is stronger than death, that solidarity is stronger than armed might, and that people—children, women, and men—matter. It is also the experience of learning from the poor, of sharing in their blessings, and of being liberated by them.

In spite of this, spirituality has often been misrepresented and misunderstood. For many it refers to something ill-defined, vague, and nebulous. Or it smacks of monastery and asceticism; it is too high and ethereal, far beyond the reach of ordinary human beings and day-to-day life. It is felt to be essentially immaterial, its realm being the interior recesses of the heart, and its concerns other-worldly. It has been defined in terms of religious acts, devotions, and pieties. Spirituality has thus come to be looked upon as world-negating, non-historical, non-political, and hence as something private, subjective, and pacifying; it has to do with an important segment, but a segment of life, and is unrelated to the rest. This restrictive, reductionist, and dualist view of spirituality we reject.

Neither are we satisfied with neutral descriptions that present spirituality as the way one lives one's life; or the way one orders one's loves; or as the ensemble of one's values, views, assumptions, and attitudes. We do not wish to make the word available to Hitler as well as to Gandhi, or applicable as much to consumerism as to revolutionary striving. Spirituality for us is bound up with life and all that life involves: freedom and food, dignity and equality, community and sharing of resources, creativity and celebration of the God of life and liberation. Spiritual is all that the Spirit of God originates, gives, guides, and accompanies; all that the spirit can bless, accept, and work with. It is all that can contribute to the balance and blossoming, the healing and wholeness of India, of the human race, the earth, the cosmos. It may be described as the *Godwardness* of life, the experience of seeing God in all things and all things in God; or, as a sustained search for meaning, depth, transcendence, and comradeship, overcoming mental and social inertia and determinisms in order to grow in freedom and to be able to relate to reality.

In order to comprehend the diverse spiritual currents that crisscross India's lifescape, the religious no less than the secular, we would describe spirituality in terms of openness and response-ability vis-à-vis reality. The grace of God and the *prasada* of the Lord making openness and response possible are presupposed to be always present to every human heart and human group everywhere. The reality in question embraces everything from sand and stone to grass and dew drops, to birds and birdsongs, to human beings, their hearts and creations to the ultimate mystery we call God. Openness is letting reality come, enter, invade, touch, speak, challenge, upset, and move us to awareness, to joy, to sorrow, to tears, to anger, to action.

Contemplation is an aspect of openness, be it contemplation

of nature or of history, be this biblical history or contemporary history. In nature-contemplation begins a concern for environment, and a respectful approach to the earth as the basic sacrament of God. History is contemplated to discern the signs of the times, what God is doing in our days, and to what collaboration God is summoning us. Contemplation may, in fact it must, deepen into probing and analysis of social reality with a view to finer response. If openness is a first response and contemplation, its continuation to action is its culmination. Openness is openness for action; if no action is put forth, openness, and therefore spirituality as well, may be presumed to have been nonexistent.

It goes without saying that the response must be relevant. If it does not correspond to the need at hand, to the cry of the situation, to the call of God that comes through the people, it is no response at all. In the Samaritan story, what the two religious men did is no response, even if they hurried to the temple to pray for the man who was broken and left on the roadside. Response should also be as adequate as possible, even as the Samaritan's was. But were the Samaritan to meet with more and more such cases in his subsequent journeys along that road, would he not go beyond the relief work described in the narrative, and investigate the root cause(s) of the malaise and try to tackle these? If love is the heart of spirituality, then its concrete form, relevant and adequate, is defined not by abstract theologies and ready-made religious rules, but by the cries, needs, and possibilities of those dispossessed and cast aside on the highways of history.

The voices of those cast aside can never be totally suppressed, because from the midst of their cries for identity and humanity there emerges a spirituality that sustains them. The *dalits* and tribals have lost much of their own spiritual heritage when their historical roots were distorted by the dominant power of the majority group who tried to assimilate all minority identities within its fold. Much of this spirituality, therefore, is unrecorded, as they were basically oral traditions. However, their songs, dances, folklore, poetry, art, and drama unfold a wealth of spirituality that is yet to be explored. Archeological evidence and popular religious experiences also provide scope for this search for a spirituality that has provided to *dalits* and to tribals

the energy to survive centuries of oppression. In their new movements for identity and selfhood, founded on their traditional
value systems of justice and freedom, with a close affinity to
creation, this deep spirituality once again finds expression and
must be recognized.

From the perspective of the new spirituality that is emerging,
we also recognized the wealth of the traditional spirituality of
our land. In India in every philosophical and theological tradition, the spiritual has to do with realization of authentic Self
(*atmasaksatkara*). *Atman* is personal self, akin to absolute
Atman. Spirituality is this kinship, this imagehood, which is both
a gift given and a task to be accomplished. The self is to be
cultivated and developed (*samskara*), deepened and refined
through the four states (*asrama*) of life: life as a student, as a
householder, as a recluse having time to ponder and sift a life-
time of experiences, and as a mature person with a wealth of
insights, at the service of the world. Throughout the journey,
the goal, the lodestone of life is *moksa*, liberation from the illusions and anxieties, the pains and deaths of existence. On the
way the two spheres of value and action are *artha* and *kama*,
production and reproduction, two engagements in which one
interacts intimately with the earth and with society. This worldly
involvement is spiritual (*adhyatma*) to the extent that it is suffused and ruled by *dharma*, ethics, religion, duty, and tradition,
which orient it toward *moksa. Dharma*-ruled economic, political,
and social activity are means (*sadhana*) of spirituality. *Dharma*
is, perhaps, the most suitable Indian equivalent of spirituality,
free of the dualistic connotation of the latter.

The way of *dharma* is threefold. There is *jnana*, insight,
enlightenment, wisdom, born of meditation that discloses the
illusory (*maya*) character of the world of phenomena (*vyava-
harika*) and transports one to the real world (*paramarthika*),
where one realizes and enjoys one's union-identity with the
Absolute. For those not capable of walking this lofty path, there
is the way of *karma*, action. Originally this meant complicated
and costly ritual and sacrifice. The *Gita* interpreted it to mean
historical action in confronting injustice and doing selflessly, as
God does, the work required to hold the world together (*loka-
samgraham*) and to ensure the well-being of every creature

(*sarva-bhuta-hiteratah*). But the people's path, universal, easy, and sure, is the way of *Bhakti*, surrender, devotion, and love that responds to the love, grace, and fascination of a self-revealing personal God. The *Gita*, available in all languages and with commentaries, seeks to integrate the three paths, according primacy to Bhakti, urging struggle against enthroned and structural evil, and inviting to a vision of the world and history as realities unfolding within the Mystery of the Lord. The authenticity of vision and experiences is measured and guaranteed by the down-to-earth outcome of it all, namely, the readiness to do God's will and word in history.

We are partial to the *Gita* because it has become in some measure the people's text, and could become such in still larger measure. It is a theology and a spirituality of liberative action. It has played a significant role in India's independence movement, having inspired several leaders and being commented upon by them. We are partial to the spirituality of the people, the deprived masses, and the most oppressed groups. Some of it has been expressed and sung by the people's saints like Tukaram and Namdev.

We appreciate the new and dissenting path trailed by Gautama, the Buddha, with his rejection of caste and gender discrimination, his attack on greed, his accent on historical existence as against the mythological, his turning from esoteric books and languages to people of flesh and blood, his measureless comparison and respect for life that deeply touched and transformed for a while an emergent culture of violence and complicated ritual technology. E. F. Schumacher speaks of Buddhist economics born of a Buddhist way of life "just as the modern materialist way of life has brought forth modern economics."[3]

> While the materialist is simply interested in goods, the Buddhist is mainly interested in liberation. . . . The keynote to Buddhist economics, therefore, is simplicity and non-violence. From an economist's point of view, the marvel of the Buddhist way of life is the utter rationality of its pattern — amazingly small means leading to extraordinarily satisfactory results.[4]

Trevor Ling maintains that "the original Buddhist goal, *nirvana*, was the restoration of healthy conditions of life here and now, rather than in some remote and transcendent realm beyond this life."[5] We are partial to the spirituality or *dharma* operative in this tradition. We affirm the Sikh spirituality of service, community, and hospitality, the Sikh refusal of gender distinctions and priestly hierarchies, and the tradition of doing things and governing themselves democratically.

We wish to make our own the spirituality of the Qur'an in which God is invariably the merciful, the compassionate, and therefore enjoining mercy and compassion on all of us. We vibrate to the Prophet's call to the oppressed to fight against oppression, his stress on literacy, and his vigorous attack on ignorance and on contemporary Arab abhorrence of knowledge. We appreciate the Qur'an's openness to and respect for all religions, its concern for equality of all persons, sexes, nations, and tribes, as well as its emphasis on social justice together with total rejection of usury, sharecropping, and accumulation of wealth. We wish always to remember that Muhammad was basically engaged in liberating the weaker sections of society.

Therefore, as Indians, our search for a spirituality of liberation must preserve the liberative intuitions and values enshrined in the manifold religious traditions that are an integral part of the Indian context. Contemporary Indian spirituality must be dialogical, affirming the complementarity of different religions.

Originative religious experiences were creative responses to the felt problems of a community. However, we recognize that in its ongoing tradition every institutionalized religion tends to dilute, domesticate, routinize, degenerate, corrupt, and compromise the originative religious experience. It is manipulated and exploited to subserve the selfish, unspiritual interests of the powerful and the dominant. It is also unfortunate that the vast masses of the believers uncritically and credulously internalize the slanted and selective images and interpretations preached by the hierarchs and the clergy.

An enlightened search for liberation spirituality demands that believers sift the authentic from the inauthentic, the perennial from the relative, the essential from the accretions. Therefore it is only in critical and creative hermeneutics that religions can become liberative in the present world.

Therefore the Bhakti movement in Hinduism and the Sufi movement in medieval Muslim India are landmarks in our people's search for a liberative spirituality. Here they see religion as a community rather than as an organization, as an experience rather than as established tradition, in opposition to the oppressive sacrificial, ritualistic systems, sterile intellectualism, and repressive and exclusivist hegemony of the dominant castes.

We affirm popular spirituality and religiousness that are not power-ridden nor overly institutionalized. In doing this we continue the mind and manner of Jesus who was partial to small people and the oppressed masses. Jesus affirmed children and women, he defied traditions and rule, he mingled with outcasts, associated with sinners, and brought health to the sick and the broken. He shocked the virtuous by declaring that despised tax collectors and prostitutes could enter God's Kingdom before the elite and the powerful. Everyone had to become open and responsible like children to qualify for the Reign of God. Jesus gave thanks to God for disclosing to unlearned little ones the saving news withheld from the learned and the arrogant. The gospel is given into the hands and hearts and lives of the poor. It is from them that others have to receive it. It is by Mary of Magdala that Peter and John are evangelized with the foundational good news of the resurrecting of Jesus from the dead.

The Vision of a New World Order

It is clear to us that integral to our search for a new spirituality is a vision of a new human and humane social order that demands the restructuring of society on an entirely new basis. It is a vision that calls for a safeguarding of the unique diversity of India and demands an organization of society in which there is economic, social, political, religious, and cultural space for all who people this land. We will strive to preserve this diversity, where all people will blossom and strengthen the essential unity of India and the rest of humankind.

This vision will reject the present capitalistic organization of society and the development model that India has opted for and which is based on the exploitation of creation and of human labor. The principal motivating force of the present organization of society is private gain and profit, which in turn oppress and deprive the masses of the toiling people.

Our future society will be based on the principle of community ownership and control of all resources and democratic organization of society with collective leadership, drawing inspiration from our traditional tribal societies. Such a society can only be brought about by the devolution of economic, political, social, and cultural power down to the village level, wherein the most oppressed and disinherited will be able to decide their destinies and will be able to live life to the full in harmony with oneself, with others, and with nature. Only such a structure will ensure that the *dalits*, the tribals, the deprived castes, the oppressed minorities and nationalities, and women can wrest for themselves justice that has long been denied to them.

Our vision is beautifully expressed in Rabindranath Tagore's lines:

> Where the mind is without fear
>   and the head is held high,
> Where knowledge is free,
> Where the world has not been broken up
> into fragments by narrow domestic walls,
> Where words come out from the depth of
>   truth,
> Where tireless striving stretches its arms
>   towards perfection,
> Where the clear stream of reason has not
> Lost its way into the dreary desert land of
>   dead habit,
> Where the mind is led forward by thee into
>   ever-widening thought and action,
> Into that heaven of freedom, my father, let
>   my country awake.

Our vision is born of a new consciousness concerning people's struggles and their histories. These we view from the perspective of the oppressed masses themselves. In them we sense the promise and the process of a finer and more human future. The vision grows in clarity and significance as we strive together to embody it in our history and our day-to-day life. We know that the vision is countercultural and subversive. It seeks to open prisons, to remove blinds from eyes and let people see reality; to break down divisive walls and set the downtrodden free. It speaks of a community of women and men, equal and free, who can celebrate life with an unfragmented and wholesome earth and the God of the earth. It is sure, therefore, to clash with principalities and powers and their class systems that need prisons and that can only survive through oppression and fraud.

The vision thus implies a spirituality of conflict. It calls for a spirituality for combat — one that is to mature into a spirituality of "poetry," of untrammelled joyful creativity. To use Christian imagery, we are for a spirituality of the cross unfolding into a spirituality of the resurrection.

It will be a spirituality that says clearly that the peace traditionally associated with it could never be a cheap and shallow peace. True peace will be Easter peace which grows, lotus-like, out of the stress and strife, the darkness and the mess of Good Friday. The spirituality of those who work for a new India, a new earth, will always seek "the strength never to disown the poor or bend [our] knees before insolent might." It will not look for immediate success in the market sense of the term, but will see the struggle itself as victory in process, and recognize a new bud of life in every "no" to oppression. With the fourth Gospel, it will identify the cross as "exaltation" because the cross of Jesus is a clear affirmation, in the face(lessness) of every oppressive power, of the freedom and dignity of all the crucified women, children, and men of history. Our spirituality will consist in ever fuller openness, responsiveness, and care for everything the Spirit of life brings into being in nature or in our hearts or in history; to every event the Spirit makes and unfolds; to every upheaval through which the Spirit moves our world forward to its final liberation and completion.

Notes

1. EATWOT members who contributed to this essay on Indian spirituality include Stella Baltazar, Stella Faria, Aruna Gnanadason, Crescy

John, A.P. Nirmal, Mirmal Minz, and Samuel Rayan.

2. Siddhas or Cittars in Tamil are wandering *sanyasis*, whose earliest forerunner, Tirumular, could be ascribed to the sixth century C.E. They belong to "the anti-Brahmanic cycle" of compositions in Tamil literature. It is a living tradition. In medieval times, almost all writers on medicine, astronomy, magic, alchemy, astrology, Tantra, and Yoga were grouped together as Siddhas.

3. E. F. Schumacher, *Small Is Beautiful: Economics as if People Mattered* (San Francisco: Harper & Row, 1975), 50.

4. Ibid., 54.

5. Trevor Ling, *The Buddha-Buddhist Civilization in India and Ceylon* (n. p., 1973), 136.

6

A Philippine Search for a Liberation Spirituality

Philippine Preparatory Group[1]

Case Studies of Philippine Religiosity

The Cordillera Story

> Our homeland is rich,
> forests and mine sites,
> rice terraces and fields
> source of life.
>
> In Benguet began the dams,
> the logging concessions, and the mines;
> it was the poor who suffered;
> they were driven from their homeland.
>
> In Bontoc, our homeland,
> our land taxes are high.
> They told us they would start building a
>   dam
> that would drown our villages.
>
> Our home in Apayao
> was taken from us by the rich;
> they used bombs and bullets.
> Their abuses were terrible.

> In our homeland, Ifugao,
> the people are neglected.
> Money meant for projects
> is pocketed by politicians.
>
> Our brothers in Kalinga
> will fight for their inheritance;
> they will not permit
> the flooding of their homeland.
>
> Our homeland, Kaigorotan,
> must be fought for;
> let us unite so that we can defend
> our homeland Kaigorotan.[2]

These verses from a traditional song form called *salidumay* express the struggle for wholeness of life of the Igorots, the Kalingas, and the Bontocs — indigenous people who live in the Grand Cordillera mountain range, the backbone of northern Luzon. The story of their struggle for life and wholeness constitutes one of two cases that begin our Philippine country report.

All aspects of their life, the problems they face, and the communal decisions they make are popularized in the *salidumay* to which the people spontaneously add verse upon verse as new circumstances arise. The above verses express a call to unity to oppose the forces that threaten their way of life and bring death to their race.

Without consulting the people, the Marcos government decided on the Chico River Basin development project in 1975, involving the construction of four huge dams along the Chico River. This would have submerged almost three and one-half square kilometers of the people's ancestral lands and burial places, inundated their rice terraces, destroyed farms and other sources of cash income, and deprived them of hunting grounds and many blessings of the Chico River. Worse, it meant the displacement of one hundred thousand Bontocs and Kalingas and their virtual extermination as a people.

The people employed various means of protest, from writing

letters to the President to dismantling the tents that housed the construction equipment and carrying the equipment to the governor's office some forty kilometers away. The heavy work was done mostly by the women of the community. In his response to the government officials, Macli-ing, the martyred Kalinga leader and spokesperson of the people's opposition, captured the heart of the Kalinga position:

You ask . . . to see our titles and documents of ownership. Such arrogance to speak of owning the land when we instead are owned by it. How can one own the land when one is outlived by it? Only the race owns the land because the race lives forever.

Apo Kabunian, Lord of all, gave us life and the world in which we live. And where shall we obtain life? From the land. To work the land is an obligation, not merely a right . . . The land is a grace that must be nurtured. To enrich it and make it productive is the eternal exhortation of Apo Kabunian to all his beloved tribespeople. From its womb springs our Kalinga life.

For this, Macli-ing sacrificed his own life. Before his death, he exhorted his people:

The question of the dam is more than political. The question is life — our Kalinga life. Apo Kabunian, the Lord of us all, gave us this land. It is sacred, nourished by our sweat. It shall become more sacred when it is nourished by our blood.

The killing of Macli-ing was a powerful lesson to the mountain people who agreed to continue the struggle. In June 1980, one hundred Bontoc and Kalinga representatives signed a petition in their own blood outlining conditions for peace in the Chico River valley, among them the termination of the dam project. Moreover, they stated that the people's right to speak and be heard, and to choose their destiny and enjoy due process before the law must be upheld.

The government finally abandoned the project. The people

were victorious! They had tapped their own liberating and transforming potential rooted in their very spirituality and tradition,
in their own supportive systems and social structures.

The sacredness of all things, reverence for ancestors, and
belief in and fear of the spirit-guardians of nature, all of which
are connected with land, are the main features of the primal
religion of the Cordillera peoples expressed in their rituals. The
land is the inheritance of the living that they must care for as
they care for the remains of their dead. Neglect of this task
makes the people accountable to the spirits, who may bring sickness and misfortune as a punitive measure. Allowing their lands
and burial places to be inundated would greatly displease the
dead who would forever haunt the living.

Even political institutions of interaction and control are
closely connected with the land. The peace pact (*bodong*) defines
territorial boundaries and areas of sovereignty and independence. Traditionally, the peace pact involves only two villages in
any given ceremony. During the Chico Dam crisis, the *bodong*
was used to foster unity and interdependence among all the
tribes beset by a common problem.

Thus land is precious and central to our indigenous peoples
in their quest for wholeness of life. As expressed in a verse of
a *salidumay*:

> The problem of the Kalinga is
> reason enough to die
> for the land of the Kalingas
> is the source of life and survival.

The San Fernando Experience

Our second case study centers on the people in San Fernando, Bukidnon. A town of forty villages with a population of
forty thousand people, San Fernando is situated in central Mindanao in the deep south of the Philippines. Its people are mostly
rural peasants.

Before World War II, only the *lumad* (the tribal people of
Mindanao) lived there. Migrants from central Philippines and
northern Mindanao went to San Fernando only after the war.
Most of them were landless peasants from lowland Christian

communities hoping to acquire their own land to till. At the same time, logging concessionaires were interested in penetrating this area because of its tropical forests. Logging was a lucrative business as the country was then supplying Japan with wood for reconstruction. From the late 1940s to the 1960s, logging operations built roads going into San Fernando. As forests were leveled to the ground, the *lumad* retreated to the mountains and the lowland people, the *dumagat*, took over the cleared areas and cultivated them as rice and corn fields.

The logging operations of two companies continued till the 1980s. Given the get-rich-quick mind-set of the concessionaires, the corruption of the government bureaucracy responsible for monitoring reforestation, and the connivance of military men in the payroll of the concessionaires, nothing was done to reforest the bald mountains. In time, the peasants sensed the impact of ecological imbalance. Soil erosion became prevalent. Floods occurred regularly, even with slight rains. The people gradually traced these problems to the disappearing forests.

The parish priest and the church workers also sensed this phenomenon. Earlier, they had established basic Christian communities (BCC) among the *dumagat* in the villages. This led to the formation of lay leaders, both men and women, who also became symbols of unity as the people sought solutions to their common problems.

In 1987, the ecological problem worsened and the people were convinced the logging operations had to stop. But they knew they faced a formidable enemy, for the loggers had the full backing of the military, the courts, and the local government. They knew it meant a major risk to show their opposition to the continuing destruction of their forests.

Consolidation of the BCCs became necessary. The leaders saw the need of empowerment sessions if the people were to be called upon to support mass action. Together with the parish priests and church workers, the lay leaders were able to help the people to acknowledge the sacredness of the forests by tapping the people's belief in the spirits that live in trees and the world of nature, and to see the link between God's presence in creation and the need to protect this gift. In their Bible-sharing sessions, the people affirmed the sacredness of creation as God's gift. Destroying the gift is desecrating God. God's face is seen only through what is seen in nature, so to destroy nature is to destroy God's face. The people started to invoke popular saints such as San Isidro Labrador to help them stop the depletion of the forests with its dire consequences for the harvests and people's health. The people rely on these saints in times of sickness, pestilence, and plague. With the help of the lay leaders, the people's prayers, novenas and Mass petitions began to include ecological concerns.

Together with all this went an ecological education program that provided the BCCs with an understanding of how the eco-systems operated in the environment. Ecology became an integral part of their pastoral education, together with christology and ecclesiology. Because of the conscientization that took place and was deepened by prayers, Bible sharing, and liturgical celebrations, the people decided to picket the logging operations. The first demonstration took place in July 1987, aimed at stopping the operations of C. C. Almendras Enterprises, whose concession totaled almost forty thousand hectares. During the month-long picket, the people barricaded the streets with their bodies so that the logging trucks could not pass. The military and local police came to truncheon and arrest them in an attempt to break the barricade. But the people persisted with the picket until the government was forced to stop the logging operations.

Every night during the protest, the people gathered for Bible sharing, praying, and singing liturgical songs. As in Edsa, where the people's uprising in February 1986 took place and put an end to Ferdinand Marcos' regime in the Philippines, the people held icons, candles, and rosary beads. When their prayers were answered, they offered a thanksgiving Mass.

In November 1988, the people organized a second picket, this time against the more powerful El Labrador Lumber Company, which had a concession of over seventy thousand hectares. This time, they went to the capital and sought the solidarity of other towns to effect a total logging ban for the whole province. There was no stopping the people once their awareness of ecological issues was deepened, despite the hunger, fear, and harassment that faced them at the barricades. They knew they could succeed only with organized force and full trust in God. Once more, they had their prayer sessions and Bible sharing at the barricades. They felt assured that, given their belief in God, they had the saints and the spirits, the bishop and the priests on their side. With confidence in such support, the people kept to the barricades until they finally succeeded in their goal.

Philippine Religiosity

The preceding case studies reflect the liberation struggles going on in the Philippines — people trying to survive, people striving for a full human life.

All human beings have the basic right to life, security, and self-determination. They have an innate aspiration and drive to promote, enhance, and attain wholeness of life in all aspects — economic, political, and cultural — as part of their inherent dignity. This aspiration for wholeness is God-given, and its attainment is meant for the here and now.

Thus human beings struggle when their life, freedom, and security are threatened, or when they are denied access to the means of attaining their wholeness. The concrete life situation of the people in the Philippines, or in the Third World in general, is one of struggle to survive and to obtain the basic necessities of life. It is also a struggle to liberate themselves in the political and cultural spheres by opposing structures and forces that do not promote wholeness of life. The social dimension of the struggle gives it added strength.

The earth, the universe, and all creatures are interdependent and interrelated parts of a whole. Our indigenous communities retain this closeness to the whole of creation and value this interrelatedness and interdependence of the whole cosmos. Their ancient culture and religious traditions have a liberating potential that they have tapped and unleashed in their struggle for basic rights from precolonial times. In our present search for a liberation spirituality, we find many liberating potentials rooted in our indigenous people's culture, religion, and traditions. These liberating potentials, often untapped, are part and parcel of Philippine religiosity. To appreciate them more fully, we need to delve into the different elements or influences that have contributed to the makings of Philippine religiosity.

Philippine Indigenous Religiosity

An analysis of Philippine religiosity reveals several main aspects. Our indigenous religiosity is based on animism, which posits the existence of a spirit world and attributes "indeterminate auras emanating from certain objects of nature."[3] Rooted in pre-Spanish colonial times, it is found among unhispanized, unchristianized, and unislamized indigenous peoples, such as the Bontocs and the Kalingas in northern Luzon. It can be said to be the matrix of Philippine popular religiosity in beliefs and traditional practices.

Indigenous or aboriginal religion is part of the people's cultural tradition, along with cosmogenic beliefs, myths, and legends that have been transmitted orally in epics and other cultural forms as well as in worship rituals. It is not a fully integral system of beliefs, as it is made up of cultural layers, foremost among which are Malay animism based on the sense of an active interaction between human beings and spirits of the natural environment, such as ancient trees, and the precolonial influence of Hinduism, Buddhism, and other Asian religions on spiritual concepts.

The interaction of humans and the spirit world includes transference of supernatural powers onto objects called *anting-anting* (native amulets), rituals of healing and appeasement, rites of passage, magic formulas and incantations, and animal and food sacrifices. Ancestor worship is also an aspect of indigenous religion that has deep respect for burial grounds and elaborate rituals surrounding the dead in order to guarantee their immortality.

The concepts influenced by the Asian religions include *diwa*, *budhi*, *bathala*, and *diwata*, concepts referring to spiritual powers. However, their original meanings have been modified by Spanish colonialism and their christianized meanings rigidified in the dictionaries of the friars. For example, *budhi*, now translated as "conscience," had a broader meaning having to do with spiritual enlightenment.

Our precolonial history indicates relative egalitarianism in the people's religious practices and rituals, as well as in their social and public life. Women were not only able mothers and rulers, but even priestesses called *babaylan*. The *babaylan*, religious leaders who functioned in healing and in the performance of rites, were mostly women. However, by the mid-seventeenth century, a significant recomposition took place, with male *babaylan* often functioning as both religious and political leaders. During the many uprisings of this period, it was mostly the *babaylan* who led the revolts, and all of them were male.

Some recent studies on native revolts reveal other characteristics of indigenous religiosity, a subtle blending of "this worldliness" and magicality, which is summarized by one writer as follows:

This "third worldly" orientation of Philippine religiosity is evident in the absence of any concept of fall and afterlife in aboriginal native consciousness. More, this "this worldliness" reveals itself in the Filipino stress on the life breath located in the stomach (*ginhawa*) and in their calculating and manipulative attitude toward spiritual powers. It would seem that the appearance of groups having an "other worldly" or transcendent religious orientation was a differentiation that resulted from later Spanish and American colonial impact. Thus alongside the magical this-worldliness of Philippine religiosity are religiosities with an other-worldly orientation, e.g., that of the elite for whom the adoption of Catholicism was a point of consolidation as a class in the late nineteenth century and that of fundamentalist groups.[4]

Catholic Christianity as Taught by the Institutional Church

The Catholic faith was transmitted to the people mostly in the churches after Sunday Mass during the early years of Christianization, in the schools through catechism and religion classes in later years up to the present time, and, more recently, in Bible studies as well. Many teachers of religion have been foreigners belonging to the different religious orders established in the country mostly during the Spanish period. The schools founded by these religious congregations catered mainly to the elite, so today it is generally members of the urban middle and upper classes who are imbued with orthodox Catholic teaching. However, although these middle and upper classes have been taught to dismiss "folk religion" as superstitious, many accept or condone a number of "popular" religious beliefs and practices, mainly those that have been allowed or tolerated or even promoted by the official church. Among these are the *aras* and the veil and cord ceremony within the marriage rites, the *pamisa* (offering Masses for the dead), and many Lenten customs and rituals, such as the *pabasa ng Pasyon* (an interpretation of the passion narratives from the perspective of the elite). These middle- and upper-class Catholics are basically conservative and even referred to themselves as *katoliko sarado* (closed Catholics) during the American period in reaction to the growing Protestant influence.

Popular Religiosity in the Rural Areas

Because they have little or no access to the many opportunities concentrated in the urban centers, peasants in the rural areas who constitute the majority of the population practice a "folk Christianity," which is a syncretic blend of Spanish Catholicism and indigenous religiosity. This blend gave rise to new forms, such as the *sinakulo* (dramatic portrayal of the passion accounts), *panatas* (pledges or promises), and the *fiestas* (patron feasts). In many cases, these were appropriations of forms of "elite religiosity" by the masses. It is necessary to view folk Christianity in its colonial context, where religion formed part of the colonial ideology that served to perpetuate colonial authority and privilege. Spanish Catholicism, as introduced in the colonial period, stressed the values of patience, long-suffering, and submission to authority—values favorable to elite interests. It also instilled a profound sense of guilt with the concept of original sin and flawed human nature. The original animist innocence became overshadowed with a sense of guilt and the necessity for expiation, punishment in this life and the next, and fear of hell; thus the many *panatas*, the public flagellations, and other practices of penance.

The qualities and contents of popular religiosity did not emerge as autonomous and complete in themselves, but arose from the feudal colonial conditions of society. In a feudal colonial context, the relationship between human beings and God is personalistic and also patriarchal, meaning that it is based on the *patria potestas* where fathers had absolute and unaccountable power over family and household.[5] This patriarchal relationship placed the masses at the base of a hierarchy that ascended through levels of colonial authority with the Governor General at the top representing the King of Spain, who in turn was divinely appointed by God. This patriarchal relationship — colonizers over colonized, masters over slaves, old over young, cleric over lay, male over female, man[6] over land — was construed to be natural and thus true for all time. In general, the Filipino people, whether from the masses or from the elite, have been imbued with this religious ideology.

The fanatical cults are an extreme expression of "folk religiosity" that emerged as early as the Spanish times. A segment of the population seems drawn to such sects and cults that appeal to their need for emotional catharsis and healing, as well as to their inclination and attraction to magic and witchcraft cosmology. The cults are an odd combination of Roman Catholicism and animism. In their practices, they are either millenarians, believing that a new millennium will come about through a cataclysmic event or revolutionary action; or revivalists, whose concept of salvation is more individualistic as opposed to the communal orientation of the millenarians. As folk religion was used to advantage by the colonial authorities in Spanish times, so today fanatical cults are still utilized by the government through the military for its counterinsurgency program, with dire consequences for the civilian population. Moreover, fanatical cults as well as other religious groups have successfully been used to implement the low-intensity conflict (LIC) strategy.

Nationalist and Populist Reaction to Roman Catholicism

A nationalist and populist reaction to Roman Catholicism, precipitated by the abuses of an exploitative "frailocracy"[7] emerged even before the Propaganda Movement and the Revolution of 1896. This rejection of the frailocracy, intensified by masonic influences and the church's image as an institution furthering colonial interests, led to the founding of the Philippine

Independent Church (PIC) and other sects that sought autonomy from Rome. This can be construed as the radical extension
of the move for secularization and Filipinization of the clergy.
The nationalist character of the PIC and other sects is revealed
in their intent to venerate Filipino heroes as saints and to choose
their own bishops who would work for the interests of the Filipino people. The populist character is seen in the PICs and the
sects' espousal of the interests of the masses as against those of
the dominant classes.

The religiosity of the PIC, particularly in its early stage, was
a nationalist reaction not only against the Roman church but
also against American colonization. This can be gleaned from
the early liturgical life of the PIC in the realm of religious stat-
ues, vestments, hymns, and prayers. The best known religious
statue is the *Birhen ng Balintawak* (Our Lady Virgin of Balintawak). There are actually two images in the statue: the Virgin,
in a gown designed after the Philippine flag, symbolizing the
mother country, and a young boy, garbed as a Katipunan gue-
rilla, representing the struggling Filipino people. On the original
statue, an inscription is written: *"Ama ko, sumilang nawa ang
aming pagsasarili"* (My Father, may our freedom come). In the
early American period, clear violations of the Anti-Flag Law of
1907 were manifest when the PIC started playing the national
anthem as the bread and wine were elevated at Mass, and dis-
playing the Philippine flag on the altar, in order to remind the
people of their continuing desire for independence.

Besides the PIC, other sects and cults showed the same
populist and nationalist thrust. For example, the *Cofradia* sect,
founded in 1832, attracted mostly peasants and was already seen
as anti-Spanish. Situating itself on Mount Banahaw, which is
considered a sacred mountain, the sect confirmed its nationalist
bent when it linked up with the revolution against Spain in 1896.
Today, Mount Banahaw is home to a new sect, the *Samahanang
Tres Personas Solo Dios*. Founded in 1936, it carries the nationalist and populist traditions of the *Cofradia*. While its religiosity
is markedly pre-Christian with many practices assimilated from
the Aeta aborigines, the *Samahan* claims to be a Christian sect.
One unique feature of the *Samahan* is its all-women priesthood,
which reflects the more egalitarian tradition of precolonial

times. The priestesses administer the sect's four sacraments, lead the prayers and religious ceremonies, and go to many parts of the country on regular "mission" during which they perform a two-hour liturgical dance full of religious and patriotic hymns.

The Protestant Influence Brought by the American Period

Protestant churches were introduced by American missionaries at the beginning of American colonial rule. In their teachings, the missionaries emphasized the values of sacrifice, suffering, and service, thereby reinforcing the passivity of the common people. At the same time, the Thomasites, a group of American educators, transmitted religious and cultural ideologies that backed the "American way of life" and values that ensured American economic and political interests in the colony. Studies have shown the relationship of the Protestant, particularly Calvinistic, ethic with the capitalist values of thrift and the spirit of commercial enterprise. Wealth was regarded as a sign of God's favor. This value given to material prosperity assured the political dominance of the wealthy class—the landlords, the merchants, the intellectuals—who were integrated into the officialdom of American colonial rule. A reason for the limited sway of Protestantism in comparison to Catholicism may be the absence in Protestant churches of religious images so appealing to the masses who seek concrete representations.

The Influence of Vatican II and Liberation Theology

Two trends of theological thinking and practice gradually emerging in the Philippines have influenced the people's religiosity: one trend centers around cultural identity (inculturation), and another emphasizes the present Philippine context and the need for social change (contextualization). On the one hand, there are theologians who, taking their cue from Vatican II's call for "indigenization," stress the people's culture and tradition in their effort to formulate a local theology. Sometimes this effort emphasizes the linguistic aspect of culture. On the other hand, there are progressive church people who have decided to work towards contextualization. Part of contextualization involves the study of the people's ways of experiencing and worshiping God as these people work for justice and freedom for themselves and other oppressed groups. Lately, contextualization also involves an analysis of popular religiosity so that it can take on a liberative thrust.

Other aspects of Philippine religiosity include the influence of Islam. However, this influence, limited to the southern Philippines, is not within our present competence to assess.

People's Practice Related to Popular Religiosity

For four and one-half centuries, people have held on to the practices related to popular religiosity, although some of these have been discouraged and even condemned by church leaders. Forbidden, for example, are rituals seeking favors from the *diwata*, who are considered lesser deities. Since these rituals cannot be performed with the priest's blessing, they take place outside the church with an acknowledged learned person, either male or female, performing the ritual. These rituals are usually linked to activities that sustain life, such as planting and harvesting crops, fishing, hunting, cutting trees for houses, healing the sick, and so on. More often than not, blood is shed in such rituals. Whatever is offered—chicken, pig, carabao—is shared and enjoyed by the whole community in a festive spirit, bringing forth songs, dances, and stories. Rituals to the *diwata* also include rites of passage, where nature symbols are intertwined with Christian symbols, for example, a mother dips her finger in the cup containing chicken blood and puts a sign of the cross on the forehead of a child celebrating a birthday. Central to all these rituals and practices is the belief that the *diwata* are everywhere in the environment. This involves a cosmic world view that brings together in harmony the spirit and our world, seasons and daily life, the sacred and the secular.

Though many "folk" practices are discouraged by the church, some are tolerated, such as seeking cures by wiping icons with a handkerchief. But whether the practices are tolerated or forbidden outright, people see no contradiction between performing them and remaining loyal to the Catholic church. The existence of a contradiction remains a problem from the priest's perspective, which holds that "superstitious beliefs" have no place in Christian life and prayer.

The fact remains that many popular practices occupy a central place in the church's official calendar, such as during the Christmas season, Holy Week, All Saints' and All Souls' Days, and the patron saint's feast day or fiesta. Among these official rites and celebrations, however, are extra-church practices on the same liturgical days. For example, *herbolarios* (community medicine men and women) consider Good Friday and Holy Saturday the best days to prepare herbal medicine, for at this time Jesus is dead and the *diwata* could be asked more freely to make the herbal concoctions more effective.

Other extra-church and devotional practices occur during the fiesta, especially in churches where the patron saint has a huge following or is known to perform miracles. The novena, fiesta Mass, and procession become the setting where the people seek the saint's favors for their concrete human concerns. Such supplications are considered incomplete without touching the icon of the saint, snatching flowers from the *carosas* (floats) after the procession to assure fisherfolk, for example, of a good catch, and making a *panata* or *panaad* in return for the favors. In the churches and shrines, the icons attract the people not only during the fiestas but on the day when the novenas are said, for example, to the Mother of Perpetual Help in Baclaran on Wednesdays, and to the Black Nazarene in Quiapo on Fridays.

In some regions of the country, there is a peculiar practice associated with baptism. After the rite, mothers rush their baby outside the church, for the first baby out is assured of a long life. Similarly a number of rituals, beliefs, and practices surround the healing of the sick. Icons, holy water, and the palm blessed on Palm Sunday are believed to cure the sick, as well as Latin prayers said while applying herbal medicine.

From this sampling of religious customs and practices, we can detect a "this-worldliness" and magical orientation. Often, the Filipino people are charged with having a spirituality that is too political or secular; yet the concern for the immediate here-and-now is but a manifestation of what is deeply imbedded in our culture.

In the popular practices, we see the significant role that women play. Since these practices are closely connected with the people's day-to-day living, the majority of practitioners are women, who are held responsible for the concrete nurturance of the family. It is mostly the women we see in novenas, processions, and fiestas, wiping icons, making supplications for the welfare of the family. We also see them active as *herbolarios* and as ritualists in seeking favors from the *diwata*.

Attitudes toward Philippine Religiosity

There are three main attitudes toward popular religiosity. The first aims at preservation of the traditional religious concepts and values, in some cases romanticizing them and strengthening the religious ideologies that serve the interest of the dominant classes. These attitudes are reflected mostly by fundamentalists like the Moonies and by American foundation programs that have recently made their appearance in the Philippines.

The second attitude, a minority one, is one of rejection or mere tolerance. Popular religious practices are forms of superstition and must be suppressed.

The third attitude combines respect with a critical view that aims at discerning between the negative and positive aspects of popular religiosity. The groups espousing this approach realize that accepting popular religiosity in toto will not lead to change or any liberating transformation of society, but simply perpetuate the status quo. However, they feel that some of these practices should be integrated in pastoral work. Popular religiosity indicates where people are at; if faith is to be inculturated, then the people's level of consciousness and their actual practices must be taken into account. Popular practices reflect the people's spirituality, a living sign of the people's culture and faith life. While people's religiosity cannot be romanticized, it can be a source of evangelization for pastoral workers, for it reflects the faith life of the poor; it is also an authentic source for theologians who seek a meaningful theology of and for the people. On the other hand, it can also be dangerous as it contains elements that go counter to the wholeness of life; total reliance on the power of the spirits, for example, runs counter to people power. Similarly the overrated magical potency of the *anting-anting* hinders leaders from developing organizing skills, and the tendency to respond emotionally to a crisis situation undercuts the need for rational strategies.

On the whole, popular religiosity involves both content and form, content having to do with concepts and values, and form with ritual practices and sociocultural conventions performed at designated times. To discover the liberative aspects of popular religiosity, it is necessary to identify the positive and negative aspects in both its form and its content.

Some studies in popular religiosity have identified as positive elements the following: a) its populist character, that is, arising from the masses; b) its nationalist bent, linked with an anti-colonial thrust; c) the harmony with the nature that it upholds; d) the absence of the myth of original sin, a myth that has created fear and self-abasement; e) respect for and acceptance of the priesthood of women.

On the other hand, some negative aspects that need to be transformed are: a) a false utopianism often linked with millenarianism in which only God's elite will be saved; b) the attitude of passivity and fatalism; c) the magical practices that seek no verification from reality; and d) convoluted occult notions that have induced reactionary strategies.

Pastoral workers who have seen the need to integrate the popular forms of religiosity have come up with creative alternatives that respect the positive while transforming the negative elements in the practices. For example, they use traditional symbols with new content, such as the cross with barbed wire around it, suggesting a protest against human rights violations; they combine old prayer forms, such as the rosary, with insights from contemporary biblical scholarship; they foster devotions to Mary, depicting her not so much as a docile and submissive virgin and mother but as a courageous woman who, in her Magnificat, challenged the social order of her time; they integrate the Way of the Cross with contemporary forms of protest and conscientization, such as the *lakbayan*, a people's march patterned after the Israelites' journey to the Promised Land.

Pastoral and Theological Implications

Those of us in the church who have committed ourselves to work for social transformation have had varied experiences in relation to popular religiosity. In general, most of us had a condescending attitude toward the popular beliefs and practices of our people, seeing no connection between them and the liberating work of Jesus. Many of us saw them as "superstitious," remnants of old traditional beliefs, which served as obstacles to the process of politicization and the people's struggle for liberation. Many of us did not consider them as important components of our pastoral praxis or as a source of empowerment in our justice and peace efforts.

Nonetheless, there were some of us who intuitively sensed that folk beliefs and practices were important, especially those of us who were more drawn to contemplation or who worked with people like peasants and fisherfolk who spent long hours in the fields or at sea in contemplative solitude. Those who worked with indigenous communities found themselves immersed in their cosmic world view and appreciated more keenly the natural healing of humans in close contact with the spirit world.

In time, we all began to realize that popular religiosity was an area we could not ignore or take for granted in our pastoral activities or in our effort to contextualize theology. We saw how traditional folk beliefs that are related to life and land empowered indigenous communities to take concrete action to protect their land and traditions, as in the case of the Cordillera peoples faced with the Chico Dam project. Those working with the unorganized rural peasants saw how central popular beliefs were in their day-to-day life. Their important dates were religious feasts—the town fiesta, Holy Week, All Souls' Day, and the like. Working in basic Christian communities and especially among women, we could not ignore the significance of these events.

Our assessment of pastoral and theological work and methodologies showed that we had overemphasized the political and economic dimensions of the people's life, glossing over the cultural and religious. We saw that if our perspective was to be genuinely critical and holistic, we had to know where people were in terms of their religiosity. This means viewing traditional liturgical celebrations from a new perception of symbols and myths. This means looking at the political from the perspective of the people's "this-worldly" and magical orientation. This means rereading the Edsa event in terms of the popular religiosity of the middle class, who felt empowered by the icons, candles, and flowers that they held as they faced the tanks. All this has profound implications for our pastoral and theological tasks.

Given this background, those of us in pastoral work at the grass roots as well as those involved in doing theology see the urgency of delving deeply not only into our own Judeo-Christian faith tradition, but also into popular religiosity to appreciate our indigenous religious rootings and traditions. We see its importance not only for people in the struggle, but also for those in search of a relevant Philippine spirituality. We also see as vital in our pastoral and theological work to include the insights provided by social and political scientists and historians who have done serious research in the area of indigenous and popular religiosity.

Today we find ourselves on the threshold of another exciting phase in our work for liberation. A holistic grasp of the underpinnings of Philippine religiosity becomes a vital part of our call to wholeness of life. If this is so, we cannot ignore the specific contribution women have made to Philippine religiosity. We have seen them as religious leaders in their role as *babaylan*. We have seen them taking active part in struggles for liberation and wholeness of life as in the Cordillera story. We have seen them as lay leaders of Christian communities in search for ecological balance and their community's survival. Just as we now see the important part women had in the early Christian church, so we recognize the integral role women have played in the unfolding of Philippine religiosity. We need to remain faithful to this dual heritage.

A Philippine spirituality that springs from involvement in liberation struggles—whether against economic exploitation, political repression, gender oppression, ethnic discrimination, or ecological destruction—is necessarily an integrated one. It is a holistic spirituality in touch with the movement of the Holy Spirit, not only in the people's lives but in the whole of creation. It is a spirituality rooted in our Christian faith tradition and, at the same time, aware of our animist roots that consider sacred our soil, forests, and rivers, and which are concerned with concrete bodily needs and yet also are caught up in the spirit world that has produced a richness of popular symbols and rituals. In our search for a genuinely liberating spirituality, we find a need for both an analytical and intuitive reading of reality, for both structural and cultural analysis to situate the role of popular beliefs in people's struggles, for both concrete action for justice and silent contemplation that brings forth compassion.

As we began our story with a *salidumay* that finds echoes in our hearts, so we end:

> Our Asian home is wide and rich,
> Seas, forests, mountains and fields,
> Where our sisters and brothers live,
> Where spring seeds for wholeness of life.

The call to wholeness demands that we put all things in the context of social transformation that involves the different levels at which liberation is to take place—the personal, communal, societal, and cosmic. These levels are intertwined and their interaction should produce a harmony in tune with the integrity of creation intended by the Creator.

Notes

1. Mainly the Philippine delegates to ATC III, namely, Carlos Abesamis, Rosario Battung, Bert Cacayan, Virginia Fabella, Karl Gaspar, Arche Ligo, Primo Racimo, and Elizabeth Tapia. Their report was a result of a series of in-depth discussions among themselves, in consultation with members of basic communities and resource persons in the fields of anthropology and the social sciences. Among the latter were John McAndrew of the Asian Social Institute; Mario Bolasco and Mary John Mananzan of St. Scholastica's College; and Alice Guillermo and Ponciano Bennagen of the University of the Philippines.

2. Entitled "*Ili mi'd: Kaigorotan*," this version is from a translation of the song contained in a collection produced by the Cordillera Consultation and Research Office.

3. Vicente Rafael, *Contracting Colonialism: Translation and Christian Conversion to Tagalog Society under Early Spanish Rule* (Ateneo de Manila University Press, 1983), 113.

4. See Mario Bolasco's unpublished paper, "Notes on Revolts and Popular Religiosity," written for the Philippine preparation for ATC III, in the EATWOT Asian Office in Manila.

5. See Sandra Schneiders, *Women and the Word* (Mahwah, N.J.: Paulist Press, 1986), 11–13.

6. "Man" is consciously used here not in its generic sense, but specifically as the male sex.

7. Literally, rule of the friars. Generally, it refers to the overwhelming influence of the regular orders of priests during the Spanish period in the Philippines.

7

Hong Kong: Living in the Shadow of the Third World¹

Peter K. H. Lee

Christians in Hong Kong have not paid much attention in the past to "third-world" theological thinking. Churches, church-based schools, and seminaries have too often been captives of the theological mold of the First World. Christians living in Hong Kong think of their city, which shares its border with the People's Republic of China, as being in the shadow of the Third World rather than a part of it. They view the Third World as referring to poverty and backwardness. Only recently Hong Kong residents have begun to realize that their position in the "shadows" has placed them more in the grips of a third-world experience than they had previously thought possible.

What is Hong Kong and who are its people? Hong Kong is a city, a colony, an economic miracle, one of the "Four Dragons of Asia," a ferocious and overly aggressive business community of almost six million people. The people of Hong Kong include workers who toil in factories and in construction, middle-class families aspiring to rise higher, a prosperous, well-educated élite, tens of thousands of boat people from Vietnam living in subhuman refugee camps, and some seventy thousand Filipino domestic workers. Hong Kong residents hardly think of themselves as belonging to the Third World. Yet, if being in the Third World means exploitation and oppression in certain areas of life, there are shadows of the Third World in the economic and political structure of Hong Kong—with an ensuing need for liberation.

The impressive skyline of ultramodern buildings lining both sides of the harbor and the brilliant glitter of neon lights and shop decorations in its thriving commercial centers set Hong Kong apart from the grinding poverty of third-world countries. But that is only one side of the picture. Although Hong Kong does not suffer from abject poverty, it suffers from its share of exploitation, and it is an exploitation that takes subtle forms.

Hong Kong is in its last days of colonialism. A British colony since 1842, Hong Kong is scheduled to return to the sovereignty of China as a Special Administrative Region by 1997 under the formula of "one country, two systems," as agreed upon by the Sino-British Joint Declaration ratified in May 1985. One country: the People's Republic of China. Two systems: the capitalist system of Hong Kong and the socialist economy of mainland China will exist side by side. Although there was a tacit understanding behind the designation "Special Administrative Region" that Hong Kong would enjoy a "high degree of self-government," the implementation of the formula has proven to be much more difficult than the simple words, "one country, two systems."

The Drafting Committee for the Basic Law of Hong Kong, consisting of officials from Hong Kong and the People's Republic of China appointed by the Beijing Government and heavily weighted by an ideology of paternalism, intended to limit the degree of "self-government" as much as possible. The majority of the Hong Kong members on the Drafting Committee were from the powerful financial and business sectors, and, on the whole, tended to accommodate the dominant ideology of paternalistic rule. Only a few dissenting voices wanted a more representative government for Hong Kong as early as possible.

What about the period from 1991 to 1997? The Legislative Council of Hong Kong will move slowly toward direct representation according to a formula agreed upon by the Drafting Committee. However, a representative government in Hong Kong will not be possible until well into the second decade of the twenty-first century—in spite of the original promise of a "high degree of self-government."

While the political climate in Hong Kong is not overtly oppressive, it is to a large extent a coalition between economic power and paternalistic rule. The paternalism inherent in the colonial background of Hong Kong is reinforced by the autocracy of China. Ironically, this coalition between capitalistic power and political domination is supported by the avowedly socialist government in Beijing.

Anyone who thinks that capitalism in Hong Kong and socialism in China under the "one-country, two systems" arrangement would be mutually corrective will be quickly disillusioned. Socialism in China has yet to prove its success in economic terms. People in capitalistic Hong Kong do not think that socialism in China has anything to offer. If Hong Kong residents seek business with China, it is the potential for profit that interests them. Meanwhile capitalism in Hong Kong goes from "success" to "success" with no convincing critics to check its excesses.

Shortcomings of the Hong Kong Economy

The Hong Kong social structure is highly fluid and leaves room for upward mobility. Although the educational system is "elitist," in that university degrees — admission tickets to higher pay — are limited (less than .05 percent of the population are awarded a university degree locally), yet university education is open to all who qualify by examination, irrespective of "class." In addition, the Hong Kong economy is diversified enough to allow advancement for people with a great variety of talents. While business competition is always keen, those with an entrepreneurial spirit have greater chances of success along with the risks of failure. This success-oriented ideology is reinforced by Hong Kong's active mass media. Those who achieve their goals do not seem to worry too much about their future. Some do see signs of an omen hanging over Hong Kong in the not-distant future, but before bad times come to Hong Kong, they will easily emigrate to North America, Australia, or Britain.

It is this readiness to leave Hong Kong in times of trouble on the part of those who have the means, and the upward mobility of others who feel they can "make it," that create the illusion in this success-oriented culture that the system works and anyone can become successful. Living under such an illusion, it is difficult for people to see the need for liberation.

Yet the illusion will not sustain itself forever. Sooner or later, many Hong Kong residents will have their illusions shattered on the rock of reality. A consciousness of the need for liberation will begin with those who realize that they are the victims of ill treatment and with those who sympathize with the victims. Who are the victims of the system in Hong Kong?

Exploited Become Exploiters

Mr. Tan came from China seven years ago. For three years he worked as a day laborer, earning less than U.S. $13 (exchange rate H.K. $7.75 = U.S. $1.00) per day; later he worked as a carpenter and could earn up to U.S. $23 a day. Mr. Tan never complained about his pay, but his experience showed that day-to-day employment did not provide security. During certain periods the construction trades lagged. If he was ill, he had no health insurance to pay for his medical bills and received no compensation for his sick leave. Coping with housing problems put him under severe economic strain. After waiting for more than two years in temporary housing, his family of four moved into a public housing estate where they paid a monthly rent of about U.S. $77 for a space of 250 square feet.

Mr. Tan is now earning more than before, as a small subcontractor who does carpentry work himself on the side. As a small subcontractor he must show aggressiveness and ingenuity to maintain a constant flow of contracts. He employs recent immigrants from China as cheap labor and makes them work hard. To have steady work, he must depend, in turn, on the bigger contractors. He admits that he is not aggressive enough in dealing with them. Mr. Tan was exploited as a day laborer; as a subcontractor he exploits his day workers and is, in turn, exploited by the bigger contractors. And there are thousands of Mr. Tans in Hong Kong.

Mrs. Wong is a dress-shop proprietor whose shop is in a commercial building adjacent to a second-class hotel. She rents space (less than 200 square feet) for about U.S. $75 a month, but her rent is continually raised, once 50 percent and the last time 80 percent. Her business has not caught up with this rent increase. She has two salesgirls helping her, but with the low wages she is willing to pay, there is a constant turnover. To earn enough money to pay her rent, she makes the salesgirls work long hours, keeping the shop open until late at night. She herself puts in long hours of work every day. Mrs. Wong feels she has been victimized by the landlord. At the same time, in order to maximize her profit or merely to survive, Mrs. Wong feels obliged to reduce her employees' wages and to keep them working long hours. Like Mr. Tan, Mrs. Wong is both exploited and exploiter.

On the surface, the Hong Kong economy is thriving, yet there is a general orientation of values that keeps a large segment of society from being satisfied. The ones who are already economically and socially disadvantaged feel further dissatisfied if they continue to aspire to what will always elude them. Mr. Tan and Mrs. Wong undoubtedly never intended to become exploiters themselves, but they find it impossible to survive in Hong Kong's capitalist system any other way. Mrs. Wong, in particular, is troubled at times by what she remembers from early Buddhist training. Mr. Tan and Mrs. Wong, like countless other Hong Kong residents, do not know how to assess the meaning of their victimization.

Women in Hong Kong, as in most countries throughout the world, suffer from exploitation as well. Economic well-being in this "dragon" cloaks discrimination against women in pay, employment levels, and social status. These standard forms of discrimination against women are compounded by a traditional culture with its roots in both British colonialism and Confucian patriarchalism.[2]

As in third-world countries, a consciousness of the need for liberation remains undeveloped if the meaning of oppression is not critically understood. Reflection on the meaning of liberation in Hong Kong must include liberation from exploitation, oppression, and tyranny — in short, from personal and structural sin — that prevents people from experiencing a full and humane existence.

Understanding Oppression — Tiananmen Square

It was not until 1989 that Hong Kong residents truly felt the force of oppression. It was in the heat of the student demonstrations in Tiananmen Square during the month of May that Hong Kongers realized this was a people's movement for liberation with which *they* could identify. As the People's Republic of China asserted its power over thousands of dissidents in Tiananmen Square in Beijing, the entire population of Hong Kong was shocked, grieved, and terrified. The movement took on spiritual overtones and "liberation spirituality" took on real meaning. For the first time, Hong Kong residents sensed the nature of the political dictatorship that would dominate them in less than a decade. The need for liberation was no longer just an abstract idea, but a reality that had crept very close to home.

During the 1980s, the People's Republic of China made remarkable progress in economic reform. Political reform, on the other hand, did not keep pace and resulted in a system full of anomalies. Economic growth was visible, but rigid control and inefficiency in the central government stood in the way of true development. A corrupt bureaucracy could not contain the crises in the economy or in public morality. The overheated economy led to inflation and people in all quarters complained. Students and intellectuals were the ones who saw what was wrong, and they had the courage and integrity to speak up and protest.

What precipitated a spirited student movement was the sudden death of Hu Yaobong, a former General Secretary of the Chinese Communist Party. An advocate of political reform and a friend of youth, he had been disgraced two years earlier; later rehabilitated, he again began speaking of reform. After his sudden death from a heart attack on April 15, 1989, the students organized a memorial rally for Hu. That rally led to a demonstration in Tiananmen Square for democracy and political reform in the nation. The self-disciplined students used a nonviolent approach, organized a sit-in, and requested dialogue with Premier Li Peng, who declined to meet with them. A strongly worded editorial, reportedly ordered by Deng Xiaoping, appeared in *The People's Daily* on April 26, condemning the student movement. The next day half a million people turned up for a mass rally in the square. Meanwhile students rallied in other cities, including Shanghai and Changsha.

On May 4, the seventieth anniversary of a patriotic movement in 1919 that had been led by students, students from many cities in China and from Hong Kong gathered in Beijing to join in a peaceful march. Government officials still assumed an opposition posture and refused to retract the editorial that had denounced the students. Journalists, intellectuals, and professionals soon joined in the demands for freedom and reform.

As they began a hunger strike, they were joined by over 2,000 students. Certain government officials did meet with the students, but declined their request for direct television coverage of the dialogue between the government and student leaders. Parents and friends became anxious about the strikers' health, as did the people in Hong Kong who were aroused by live television coverage of the demonstration. Finally Zhao Zhiyang, the General Secretary of the Communist Party, known to be a moderate, showed up among the students. Obviously moved, he apologized to them, "We are tardy in coming to see you." He affirmed the patriotism of the student movement and assured the students that they would not be condemned for their peaceful demonstrations and rallies.

The next day Premier Li Peng granted an interview with student representatives. The students again asked for a nationally televised dialogue and a retraction of the editorial condemnation. The premier, assuming a paternalistic posture, was obviously not ready to treat the students as equal partners in a dialogue. The meeting ended with a deeper gulf separating the students and the government. On May 20, at a meeting of the Military Affairs Committee, Li Peng referred to the student strike as a cause of social unrest and declared martial law in certain parts of Beijing. He ordered a news blackout.

In Hong Kong people followed these scenes from Beijing on television and from first-hand reports in the newspapers. Practically the entire community supported the students. An estimated one million Hong Kong residents demonstrated in the streets — undoubtedly the greatest outpouring of emotion ever witnessed in Hong Kong.

The masses in Tiananmen Square, now consisting of students from all over the nation, vowed to struggle to the end without resorting to violence. They called on Chinese people all over the world to join in a worldwide demonstration on May 28. On that day an estimated 1.5 million in Hong Kong marched, showing unusual orderliness and sympathy with their fellow Chinese.

Numerous rallies and gatherings supported the people's struggle in China for democracy and freedom. The thousands of church people who participated could not help but think of liberation theology and of liberation praxis.

Meanwhile, Zhao Zhiyang was under attack in the State Council. Although retired marshals warned against the use of force to suppress the students, the generals in power were asked to declare their loyalty. Representing seven armies, one by one they declared their support for Li Peng. It appeared that power was now concentrated in the hands of Deng Xiaoping (Chairman of the Military Affairs Committee), Yang Shengkuen (a military strong man), and Li Peng.

Trucks carrying soldiers were stopped by students and other civilians as they approached Tiananmen. When tanks began to move, they too were stopped by barricades and rows of people. The students vowed to stay in the square until the government retracted its condemnation. A few quiet days followed.

Before dawn on June 4, a long line of tanks rolled out and crashed through the barricades and charged toward the tents where thousands of students were sleeping. Hundreds of lives were crushed under the tanks. Rows of people walking hand-in-hand toward the tanks were gunned down. No one can tell exactly how many lives were lost. Although the "official" report put the death toll at thirty-six, foreign and Hong Kong reporters on the scene reported a massacre of between one and two thousand students. Eyewitnesses told of large piles of bodies being set on fire by kerosene to erase all traces of death.

Identification with People's Struggles

The students' movement is described in detail because these details have been sharply etched in the minds of the Hong Kong residents. Tiananmen Square became a turning point in thinking about Hong Kong's relationship to China. People's groups in Hong Kong quickly organized themselves into an alliance for the support of the patriotic movement in China. A similar All-Hong Kong Christian Alliance emerged spontaneously to plan and coordinate activities, including demonstration marches, prayer vigils, and a mass memorial service for the victims in Tiananmen Square.

It is important to note that the response of Hong Kong Christians to events in China was no longer confined to prayer, meditation, and personal sanctification; it grew into a passion for justice and the safeguarding of basic human rights. The Hong Kong population was one in its demand for an accelerated pace of democratization. Concern that the governing of public affairs must serve the common good moved Hong Kongers from self-interest to social responsibility.

The same enlargement of horizon was true with respect to human rights. The Chinese students were not merely concerned with their own individual rights and their part in the government, but with freedom and democracy for the whole nation. In turn they helped to broaden the social outlook of the people of Hong Kong. Overnight the student demonstration in Beijing provided a lesson in civic education that would never be duplicated by the schools. Hong Kong learned that civic responsibility must have an actual relevance but also a spiritual foundation. What had happened to the students in Beijing could happen to them some day. Freedom of speech, freedom of the press, freedom of thought, and freedom of assembly were suddenly recognized as sacred rights.

The bravery, discipline, and self-sacrificing spirit of the students also had an effect on the profit-oriented people of Hong Kong. The people in Hong Kong were lifted to a higher plane of spiritual awareness. Every school boy or girl of Chinese origin had heard the sayings, "The body may be sacrificed, but humanness is fulfilled," and "Give up life in order to gain righteousness." Now they witnessed heroic young fellow-Chinese who were living models. If they were Christians, they now vividly understood what Jesus meant when he said, "No one has greater love than this, to lay down one's life for one's friends" (John 15:13).

In addition, when the unarmed students and civilians were crushed by tanks or killed by machine guns, the Hong Kong people, along with millions of people throughout the world, instinctively sensed that a divine law had been transgressed. Tyranny had been exposed, oppression overwhelmed.

Hong Kong's Christians were called to prayer, hard wrestling with real problems, and appropriate action. They gained a more realistic understanding of Isaiah's words quoted by Jesus: "to let the oppressed go free, to proclaim the year of the Lord's favor" (Luke 4:18–19), and a new concern for the millions of fellow Chinese in the mainland. The student movement in China may have been short-lived, and the Hong Kong people's identification with it may prove ephemeral, yet the experience has given Hong Kong Christians a glimpse of the meaning of liberation.

The road ahead for Hong Kong is full of pitfalls. The Hong Kong people are actually caught in a dilemma. At first they had a strong sense of identification with the students who led the patriotic and democratic movement. After the June 4 massacre, however, Hong Kong residents became frightened about their own safety after 1997. A common reaction is to plan to leave Hong Kong as soon as possible. But if there is a massive exodus, what will become of Hong Kong? There are those who want to speed up the pace of democratization. As was mentioned earlier, almost overnight even the conservative-minded business leaders and politicians who had previously put off the democratization process wanted to see an elected representative government as early as possible. But they were soon vacillating again and the entire population remains in a quandary. Residents of Hong Kong are now faced with two problems: first, what to do in 1997, and second, how to find meaning and value in a Hong Kong that is increasingly a snarl of aggression directed toward profit and success.

Spiritual Resources of the People

The Chinese people, with some of the oldest developed cultural traditions of the world, have survived even more serious traumas in the past. In 1989, Chinese patriotism provided a tremendous uniting force that aroused feelings of sympathy and anguish over the transgression of divine laws. The Chinese of Hong Kong (and of the mainland) could find support in traditional Chinese spirituality. One important thread running back through the centuries of Confucianism, Taoism, and Zen Buddhism is *hsin-hsing*, which means "heart/mind-nature/being." The two Chinese characters together convey the concept of the heart as responsive to living reality—a concept used by Mencius (a Confucianist), Chuang-tzu (a Taoist), and Hui-neng (a Zen Buddhist). Although all three sages interpreted the *hsin-hsing* in slightly different ways, all, in the end, shared a common sense of the openness of the *hsin* ("heart/mind") to the *hsing* ("nature/being"). The *hsin-hsing* consonance or communion is in both the human person and the cosmos.

Within the Chinese traditions of Confucianism, Taoism, and Buddhism lies a vivid sense of freedom—freedom from unfulfilled striving, from outward-inward dichotomy, from alienation from nature and the world at large, from estrangement from fellow beings. Life has a wonderful sense of sanctity and wholeness.

None of these three sages was an intellectual. In the writing of Chuang-tzu, the authentic person (the *chen-jen*) has the innocence of a child, and real enjoyment and freedom come from being in tune with nature. Hui-neng was explicitly against "establishing the written scripture" and wanted to "speak directly to the human heart." Mencius wanted to see the simple virtues of benevolence and righteousness practiced by everyone, from the ruler to the commoner.

Nor were these spiritual teachers elitist. Mencius had an inordinate trust in human nature. He believed that when a ruler went against the will of heaven by failing in his moral responsibilities, the common people would know it. They, in turn, were given a mandate from heaven to choose another ruler. (Indeed, in Tiananmen Square in May 1989, students carried placards that said the regime had gone against the mandate of heaven.)

Chuang-tzu poked fun at pomposity and pretension and found oneness with humanity in its pristine simplicity. Hui-neng wanted to be free from all attachment to fame or class or privilege. These men were rare spirits, but their spiritual qualities have the touch of the common folk.

Today, however, the Chinese in Hong Kong are often far removed from what I call *hsin-hsing* spirituality. They have other preoccupations—like getting more and more things for themselves or wrapping themselves in their self-concerns. Traditional

Buddhist teachings about greed as well as Christian teachings have a great deal to say to the people of Hong Kong. Both view greed as a source of unhappiness. Acquisitiveness is set aside in the way of Christ and in the Buddha's Eightfold Path to enlightenment. Buddhism says that a main source of suffering is greed. Greed fixates the self on a certain object of possible satisfaction. But everything changes, including the self and the object of desire, so that the self—bent on reaching a certain object—is doomed to be disappointed. The unenlightened person does not realize this and is therefore unhappy, without knowing why. Only enlightenment can free one from senseless striving.

Another main source of Chinese spirituality, Taoism, advocates a spirit of detachment. For Hong Kongers, people enamored by the accumulation of wealth, Confucist and Taoist ethics, with their focus on humane values and righteousness, can become a social force.

In their eagerness to catch up with the West in technological developments, the Chinese people, on the mainland and in Hong Kong, are prone to use modern technology at the expense of human values. In their intellectual pursuits, the present-day Chinese are following the modern Western philosophical and scientific approaches that tend to separate the reasoning subject and the object of understanding. In this way, modern Chinese are spiritually impoverished (their *hsin* becomes depraved), and they alienate themselves from their original endowment with its potential for fuller humanity (they cut themselves off from their *hsing*, their vital nature). The language of *hsin-hsing* spirituality is foreign to them. This is particularly true in Hong Kong, where estrangement from Chinese culture is part of the difficulty. Modern life, in Hong Kong as elsewhere, is ridden with conflict, estrangement, and hostility.

As Christians in Hong Kong reacted to events in 1989, they experienced the suffering of students in Beijing and they were reminded by the cross that there is no easy way out of the world's troubles. The grace of the cross—Christ dying for the sake of humanity—is a costly grace, but it demonstrates completely God's love for erring and suffering humanity. For Christians, the cross is central to a spirituality of liberation.

Hong Kong residents, like people in all parts of the world,

need a spirituality that is not merely a Sunday affair, but a spirituality that is a sustaining and transformative power, both in the individual's life and in the larger social environment. In the case of Hong Kong, it means liberation from social and economic injustice, from false values and consciousness, from a paternalistic form of government. It is liberation from acquisitiveness, avarice, and excessive consumerism. It is identification with the great multitude of fellow Chinese in the mainland in their desire to be liberated from tyranny and autocracy. It is to seek the release of the students and intellectuals who have been imprisoned for their demands for reform and freedom. It is to press for responsible participation by the people in making decisions on public affairs. It is to live in a society where basic human rights are protected. It is liberation to live a more humane and holistic life for the many. Life can be sane, authentic, and free, if only people are liberated from their shackles, both outward and inward.

Christian social ethics has a powerful message to deliver if Christians turn to the concrete example of Jesus when he began his ministry. He received inspiration from the prophet Isaiah:

> The Spirit of the Lord is upon me,
> because he has anointed me to preach
>   good news to the poor.
> He has sent me to proclaim release to the
>   captives
> and recovering of sight to the blind.
> (Luke 4:18–19)

The spirit of the Lord touches us and leads us to be with the poor, the captives, and the blind. We share their suffering and anguish in a world full of inequity and injustice. In their midst, our eyes are enlarged to see God's justice and mercy. Proclaiming the good news of liberation follows naturally; it is not just preaching, but action and participation in God's power to liberate. Liberation is not merely liberation from poverty and exploitation and oppression, but also life lived in freedom and responsibility and dignity. It is no longer living in darkness but in the light.

I am reminded of another biblical passage: "But you are a

chosen race, a royal priesthood, a holy nation, God's own people, that you may declare the wonderful deeds of him who called you out of darkness into his marvelous light" (1 Pet. 2:9).

God's own people are the workers who toil in the factories and in construction work, who receive better pay than before but still lack the protection of basic social security and have little sense of their worth as human beings. Among these workers are some seventy thousand Filipino domestic helpers working for Hong Kong families. God's people are women whose status in society is less than equal to that of their male counterparts. God's people are also middle-class families and people aspiring to rise higher but living under a set of false values never fully realizable. They are the Chinese students and intellectuals who have been imprisoned because they dared to call for reform in the government. They are the billion and more masses in China living in poverty under an outmoded and inept party machinery with leaders who justify their position and power by an ideology that is on the brink of economic and moral bankruptcy. God's people are also tens of thousands of boat people from Vietnam who have fled to Hong Kong and who now live in subhuman refugee camps waiting for "adoption" by countries who will take them. God's people are Hong Kong's exploiters and Hong Kong's exploited.

Whether these people know it or not, they are God's people and should be channels of God's spiritual power. For Christians, the resurrection must always follow the cross. With the risen Christ, his followers can gather up all the spiritual treasures — Christian and non-Christian — to make life for all rich and full. The privileged will learn to share their privileges with others, openly and freely, and the disadvantaged will be aided to move from the shadows into the light of dignity and freedom. In Hong Kong and China, the liberating elements in Christian teachings and traditional Chinese teachings must work hand in hand in developing a spirituality to liberate, so Christians can echo "the wonderful deeds of God who called you out of darkness into the marvelous light."

Notes

1. This report/reflection is the result of two group processes in 1989 in anticipation of the third Asian Theological Conference (ATC III)

of the Ecumenical Association of Third World Theologians (EATWOT). The first was an informal meeting with individuals from several Christian groups, and the second consisted of representatives of several Christian organizations in Hong Kong. Parts of this paper were presented in a panel discussion at the ATC III meeting in Suanbo, South Korea, in 1989, and were subsequently revised by the author.

2. For a discussion of these issues from a Christian feminist perspective, see Christine Tse, "A Catholic Perspective," and Kwok Pui-lan, "The Emergence of Asian Feminist Consciousness of Culture and Theology," in Virginia Fabella and Sun Ai Lee Park, eds., *We Dare To Dream: Doing Theology as Asian Women* (Hong Kong: Asian Women's Resource Centre, 1989; Maryknoll, N.Y.: Orbis Books, 1990).

8

A Sri Lankan Search for a Common Vision amidst Division[1]

Sri Lankan Preparatory Group

Our Political Reality

During the last two decades Sri Lanka has witnessed a movement toward centralization of power and gradual narrowing down of space for participative democracy. This process of centralization gathered momentum with the implementation of the Constitution of 1978, which consolidated executive power in the office of the President. Elected directly by the people, the President was made supreme in all executive functions by the Constitution. The President appoints and dismisses Cabinet ministers, presides over the meetings of the Cabinet, and can even exercise executive power through aides without the participation of the Cabinet.

Although not responsible to parliament according to the Constitution, the President has power to address the parliament at will and is empowered to summon or dissolve parliament. From 1978 to 1988, with a five-sixths majority of the ruling party, the President directed the parliament, through the five-sixths majority of the ruling party, to support his plans.

The Constitution also empowers the President to appoint judges of the Supreme Court and the chief justice. Moreover, the President is immune from legal action. Many legal and extra-legal measures were used at the inauguration of the Constitution to control the composition of the judiciary.

Both the legal state apparatus and extralegal measures of violence have been instrumental in creating a system of terror to depoliticize the Sri Lankan polity. However, the authoritarian use of political power cannot continue for a long time without a serious challenge to it, for authoritarianism breeds its own opposition. The political opposition has been met with force and violence through the use of security forces and other paramilitary groups, and in this way violence has been institutionalized to prevent democratic interventions in the political process. Those who suffered most from the system were the ones to react first. Quite naturally those responses were desperate and violent.

The most effective response in the first instance came on the ethnic front. This struggle on the ethnic front aimed at creating a separate state, and thus challenged the trend for centralization of power and the very nature of the Sri Lankan state itself, which has taken the rights of minority communities for granted. The militant armed groups in the north and east of Sri Lanka responded to the violence of the state with violence. This conflict brought about an all-round crisis in the Sri Lankan polity that affected the lives of many people and created conditions for the formation of armed militancy in the southern districts of the country as well. The Sri Lankan power élite responded to the mounting crisis militarily, which resulted in the widespread militarization of the country. The consequences were not only uncontrollable bloodshed but also the diversion of scarce resources from investment and consumption to purchases of arms.

The Economic Situation

On the economic front, the policies of the government were geared to liberalize economic activities, to strengthen the market forces, and to encourage foreign direct investments and export-oriented development. Although these policies brought about economic growth in certain sectors of the economy, they failed to sustain a growth momentum. According to official sources, half the population of Sri Lanka receives food coupons. This is an indication of the failure of the economic policies to ensure "spill-over" effects of economic growth.

These economic policies, supported and guided by the International Monetary Fund and World Bank, ensured that Sri Lanka received large amounts of foreign loans, including commercial ones. Most of these funds were invested in large enterprises like the Mahaweli Ganga Development Project (a river diversion and development scheme) and Air Lanka (Sri Lanka's national carrier). Except in the area of some agricultural development and electricity generation, the benefits of these heavy investments have yet to be realized. However, the country's indebtedness to foreign sources has increased by leaps and bounds. Sri Lanka's efforts to encourage direct foreign investments through transnational corporations (TNCs) have not been as successful as expected. Most of the current foreign investment is in the area of garment production, particularly in the free trade zone, but employment generation is very slow. Presently the country is burdened with 1.2 million unemployed people.

The state sector of the economy is experiencing losses and inefficiency. Privatization of state enterprises is suggested as a possible solution for these problems. However, experience shows that problems of the state sector arise because of corruption, political patronage, and bad management.

Blind faith in the market as the regulator inhibits serious analysis of the situation. In place of serious analysis and democratic discussion of the problems, religion, religious symbolism, and cultural issues are used to manipulate the people to give false hopes of impending prosperity. This overall crisis in Sri Lanka is increasing the gap between the rich and the poor.

Economic poverty is further worsened by humiliating personal relationships between the powerful and the powerless. Because the poor depend for their daily living on the benevolence of politicians, bureaucrats, rich people, and those who serve as agents of the ruling elite, their human dignity is violated. Marginalized, humiliated, and poverty-stricken young people among the majority Sinhalese and minority Tamils have taken up arms against the state out of desperation. Though the objectives of these two groups are different, their origins are connected to the excessive authoritarian use of power by the ruling classes against the people, the inability of the Sri Lankan state to provide for the basic needs of the people, the restrictions imposed on the democratic process from time to time, and so forth.

The Ethnic Problem

Race and culture are among the mythologized aspects of human life in Sri Lanka. These two are, as it were, the individuating and the identity-giving elements of a citizen of this country. This mythologization and quasi-divinization of race and culture have not only fostered an exaggerated pride and bigotry over one's race and culture, but also a spiteful evaluation of the "other." This pride and evaluation were nurtured and fortified throughout our history by the rulers of old and now.

The mere realization that the other belongs to a "race" that is not one's own is enough to make some people become angry. People have been trained and brainwashed here to look at the person of the other race not as a twentieth-century individual, but as one who has inherited the rights and wrongs of twenty centuries. Ironically, people today seem to suffer and die on behalf of those who live no more. For the past forty years, both the government forces and the militant movements of all three races have carried out disproportionate and brutal elimination of people belonging to the other cultures and races, and even religions as well. One can name, for instance, the Sinhala-Tamil, Sinhala-Muslim, and the Tamil-Muslim ethnic and communal clashes of the various periods or decades since independence. In the first three decades, these clashes lasted but a few days or weeks. What is more discouraging and horrifying is that the last ethnic conflict that started in 1977 still continues.

The ethnic problem was aggravated by the open economic policies of the post-1977 period as well as by the political system, which was made more authoritarian to ensure the continuity of the economic policies. This centralization of power has made the ethnic conflict less amenable to solution. The proposal for devolution of power to provincial councils seems to be a step in the direction of a solution. While, for the present, the ethnic animosities seem to have lessened, the problem is by no means resolved. The presence of the Indian Peace Keeping Force in the country, which was caused by a number of complex political factors, also presents serious problems, especially regarding the country's sovereignty. This, more than ever, demands that conflicting communities come together for socioeconomic and political solutions. The future is uncertain. Even though many people realize that today's sociopolitical problem has transcended the mere boundaries of ethnicity, the ethnic question remains one of the existing components of the national problem.

Signs of Hope

Yet the pessimism of this total crisis is overshadowed by signs of hope. Crisis can also bring growth. A sinful structure can breed courage to resist. The poor, for example, are compelled to ask "Why?" in the face of tragedy. Bereavement and suffering can create a new consciousness and renewed power to resist evil. Women left alone can grow in strength. In other words, conflict can be the background for creativity. In the midst of ethnic conflict, more and more people are seeing that instead of mythologizing and absolutizing race and culture, one should relativize them and regard the various races and cultures as complementary and mutually enhancing.

Many Sri Lankans wish for justice, participation, and change. In many ways the struggle of the youth of the land is inspired by their yearning for justice and the restoration of the democratic process. However, their failure to place politics before guns has added to the spiral of violence that is brutalizing the Sri Lankan polity and adding further burdens on the poorer sections of the population.

Yet, in the face of this fact, we cannot just hold up our hands in horror and shun all forms of violence. We are compelled to understand that when all other forms of political expression are closed, when the democratic process is corrupted and the media are monopolized by some groups, there will be those who feel compelled to resort to armed action as a last resort. But our hope and our plea is that various political forces in our society will be able to confront and contest one another in a fair and free democratic process as the only alternative to the limitless violence we now experience. The present torment can be the crucible to form new structures of community and new forms of action.

It is true that the escalation of violence around us with so many people killed each day has gripped the nation in a psychosis of fear, yet this very violence has produced people of extreme courage and fortitude. While many have become afraid to take clear stands and to express what they believe, there are those of various political persuasions who have been willing to die for their convictions. Unfortunately, many creative persons who could have helped the nation out of its present crisis have been killed. All of us have lost friends of different political parties and religions, both clergy and laity. These martyrs are fulfilling an invaluable role to make a better Sri Lanka possible, and our churches should encourage such sacrificial living by example. An emerging spirituality in Sri Lanka today demands that we too be ready to lay down our lives in defense of beliefs worth this supreme sacrifice.

A Need for a New Spirituality

Our reality, our fears, and our hopes force us to ask ourselves what spirituality means for us today. Spirituality is the search for our better selves, our true selves. We want to grow into the fullness of our personality, to reach fulfillment and happiness, to share and commune with others, to be the persons God has planned and destined us to be.

We can discern at least three meanings in our understanding of spirituality. We see spirituality as the relationship of all human life to the Transcendent God who is Infinite Spirit; we must become aware of this relationship and freely accept it. We also look upon spirituality as the living out of Christian life under the influence of Jesus as the vivifying spirit of the New Covenant, the free person who frees us all. A third meaning is our understanding of spirituality as the animation, inspiration, and energizing of life under the action of the Holy Spirit, the third Person of the Holy Trinity. Traditional spiritualities have served Christian people well. At their best, they kept a balance between personal sanctification and the concern for social and secular betterment. Medieval Christian monasteries were often civilizing centers for education, social services, and the propagation of better agricultural methods. These older traditions remain fountains and wellsprings of life in all its dimensions today.

Nonetheless, it is true that there is also an individualistic and pietistic form of traditional spirituality still prevalent today. It sees the goal of the spiritual life as other-worldly salvation, freedom from sin and death. Jesus is seen only as the unique Savior who redeems us from original and personal sin, and not as a total liberator who frees us from every enslavement, including economic, social, and political servitude. This traditional form of spirituality tends to be identified with a series of devotions engaged in to bring about individualistic sanctification. It is no longer able to meet the challenges of the times.

Since the nation of Sri Lanka is in deep crisis and turmoil, a spirituality for today cannot prescind itself from conflict and struggle. Escapism from conflict resolution into a dream world of peace cannot be authentic or realistic. We must face the divisions and antagonisms in our society, whether of ethnic groups, social classes, language, cultures, or religions, and learn to overcome these conflicts from the inside.

A liberative Sri Lankan spirituality urges us to see our reality through the attitudes and values of Christ as we find them in the gospels. It urges us to transcend the narrow confines of race and culture, the determinisms of blood relationships and social discriminations, the restricting orthodoxy of religion and religious traditions, and the heavy-handedness of authoritarian structures. It urges us to respect the other; to appreciate, accept, and foster the resourcefulness of the other; to share opportunities and power with the other; to hold the others as co-responsible in the development and liberation of the country. It calls for the emergence of a truly national consciousness that acknowledges the richness and resourcefulness of plurality as a source of unity, and devolution as a means of ushering ethnic harmony and peace in our nation.

A spirituality for Sri Lanka will have to be an interfaith one. We have in our country the major living faiths of Asia — Buddhism, Hinduism, and Islam. Each of these religions has its own spirituality which can be very enriching but sometimes dehumanizing, just as our own Christian spirituality can be dehumanizing at times. We must be in constant dialogue with these religionists to learn from them how to be liberative and not enslaving. We must be open toward them and sensitive to what God is doing among them. We can learn from their cultural treasures and incorporate their techniques and methods in our own spiritual ways. The heritage of Buddhist and Hindu meditation practices is especially rich. We will find that the core values of the other living faiths come very close to our core values. Together with people of other faiths, we can set about the task of freeing our society.

Besides having different religious traditions in the nation, we have a multiplicity of ideologies, such as Marxism, democratic and liberal traditions, and a secular scientific tradition. These traditions have their own spiritualities. We can learn much from them, too, such as preferring persons to commodities and appreciating the power that comes from social solidarity. We can learn the importance of participation in the exercise of democracy, and the new horizons that open up before humankind through science and technology.

Our spirituality for today is thus incarnate in temporal realities. We have to learn to give full religious value to the secular civilizing effort of humankind. Such a spirituality is not restricted to the confines of the church and monastery but is operative in the homes, farms, factories, and schools, even though the monastic tradition has much to contribute as a critique of society and an example of contemplation in freedom.

Thus spirituality for Sri Lanka today is a spirituality of liberation — liberation understood as a freeing from the impediments to a full life, such as selfishness, the weight of riches, and the unbridled pursuit of pleasure. This spirituality evolves from and emerges in a sharing with the poor as they struggle to free themselves from the oppression of enforced poverty and misery that result from the unbridled egoism and insatiable craving of the affluent, both personal and social.

But liberation is also the freedom to pursue the full life, to tend intensely to the ultimate values of truth, goodness, beauty, and unity, which we have called Kingdom values. These are the values that spring from the beatitudes of the Kingdom (Matt. 5:3–11) and the fruits of the Spirit (Gal. 5:22–23). Wherever the values of justice, mercy, truth, loving kindness, faithfulness, compassion, reconciliation and peace are accepted and lived, there the Kingdom is growing and the Spirit of God is present.

What kind of word must a liberative spirituality address to the various sections of our society?

— To the youth struggling for a new form of society—words of faith, courage and strength to help them discover ideals of love and brotherhood/sisterhood;

— To teachers—words to give them strength to practice what they preach and courage to face rejection by authorities for their principles and convictions;

— To the poor, workers, peasants—words that will help them to overcome ignorance and hatred, and not to be lured by the wrong kind of god, such as greed, money, wealth, and pleasure;

— To those who are rich and comfortable—words to enable them to give up their abundance in a liberative kenosis and despoiling of the self, and to go out towards the poor.

A New Vision

Those who work together for the liberation of our people must share the same vision. We seek a Sri Lanka in which people of various races will be able to live with equal dignity using their languages and expressing themselves in their own cultures. We seek a state in which all persons will be able to practice their own faith while the state itself remains secular, with a just and fair attitude toward all religions. We seek a land in which we share our abundant resources, and extremes of poverty and wealth are abolished.

We seek a Sri Lanka in which all people will be able to participate in decisions affecting their lives at all levels. Men and women must be enabled to share equally in all spheres of life as co-citizens. When we allow distinctions that divide us in one area of life, it is but a short step to begin distinctions in other areas as well. It is the attitude of discriminating against other human beings on any grounds whatsoever that has caused the deep and bitter resentments among the people of Sri Lanka.

In all this, we must learn to discern the demonic in the life of the nation. Often, what appears to benefit the people may not really benefit them in the long run, and may only be the means of deceiving them for a while. Exploiting of our land by the TNCs may provide employment to our people for a few years, but when the land has lost its fertility, these corporations leave and the people are left with neither employment nor land to cultivate. This has already happened in Asia. Cramming the distribution of social benefits within a period of a few years may raise the people's hopes, but in the final analysis such a scheme may do more harm than good. Lotteries, which are a feature of our national life, dangle hopes of better times before our eyes, but they bring great riches only to a very few, while levying an imperceptible tax on the unsuspecting poor. Our people have to be enabled to save themselves from deception and realize what true human development means and entails.

The task of learning how we can achieve our own liberation is one in which we must all share. Songs, stories, and dramas of liberation can be used very effectively, and our country has no dearth of these. We must ensure that the media publicize such materials. We regret that songs capable of motivating our people in the right way are often not popularized by radio or television. The suppression of such creative material increases the frustration of our people and encourages them to express themselves violently.

There is an increasing tendency among youth who have lost hope in the system to refuse a future within the existing economic, social, and political structures. Young people have also lost faith in the ability of religions to find solutions. They do not seem to have much confidence in the approaches of religions towards social liberation, or in the ability of the present teachers of religion to work toward effective solutions. This is due to the long years of failure of the religions to work concretely for the achievement of social ideals and goals, or to adopt approaches that are real responses to the concrete operative oppressive forces. Credibility can be recovered only through a concrete rejection of what is evil in the existing structures and a refusal to submit to them as done by the first teachers, such as Jesus and the Buddha, and the early communities of disciples.

The new vision which should inspire our spirituality nevertheless comes up against a number of obstacles that prevent its full development. The first of these is the failure of the churches to impart the social dimensions of religion to the people. Our church congregations have to be taught this new vision and the insights and values that go with it, with the stress on Kingdom values. This new type of spirituality must be taught in the seminaries, the formation houses of religious men and women, and the training centers of lay leaders. Such training must go hand in hand with praxis and situational involvement with the poor, the youth, workers, and peasants.

The institutional framework of the church is another great obstacle. Youth are often driven away by the accumulated riches of the church, the heavy-handed use of authority, and the introverted concentration on church affairs. Church structures have to be constantly reformed to make the church a sign of freedom and liberation for the poor and marginalized in service to the Kingdom.

Sri Lankan popular religiosity among Christians and other religionists is often tainted with mercenary motives and a preoccupation with private, personal, and familial well-being. Religious practices and devotions springing from popular religiosity have to be purified. There are liberative trends in these forms of religion, too, but these have to be released and developed. Much study and reflection is necessary in this area.

Spirituality needs to be liberated from the fetters of the older forms to enable it to play its part in the forward march of the people toward the New Jerusalem.

Notes

1. This statement is the outcome of a consultation organized by two EATWOT members, C. R. Hensman and Sr. Marlene Perera, to formulate a Sri Lankan liberating spirituality. It was held March 9-12, 1989 at the Fatima Retreat House, Lewella, Kandy.

9

Bible Studies for a Liberation Spirituality

The Bible is at the center of Asian Christian spirituality. It is acknowledged as the foundation of all Christian traditions and serves as an indispensable base for all emerging Christian theologies and spiritualities.

When Protestant missionaries first came to Asia, they brought the Bible with them and taught it using their own languages. As soon as they learned the languages of Asians around them, they collaborated with native speakers to translate the Bible into Asian vernaculars. The churches persisted in teaching the Bible in the languages of the ordinary people and used sacred Scripture in a literacy campaign both to educate and to liberate. In this way, the Bible not only helped Asian peoples to read and write; its stories also served as a source of political inspiration. Thus, in Asia, the Bible has been one of a few books that provided liberating ideas to ordinary people.

On the Catholic side, though Scripture reading was not popularized until the present century with the impetus given by Pope Pius XII's encyclical *Divino Afflante Spiritu* in 1943, Catholics have been familiar with biblical stories from the time of the earliest missionaries. Along with Christian doctrine and devotions, missionaries brought with them accounts of biblical events and personages for the people's inspiration and emulation. In the present times, the multiplication of Bible translations into Asian languages, the rapid growth of Bible-study groups, and the wide use of the Bible in basic ecclesial communities as well as for personal reading and edification show the deep appreciation and reverence Asian Catholic faithful have for the word of God.

While all Christian communions recognize the treasure that is contained in Scripture, it is important to note that Asian Christians have also been led, albeit unintentionally, to misunderstand and misuse the Bible by Western missionaries who taught the people to read the Bible with Western eyes and interpret it from Western perspectives. More often than not, this "orthodoxy" directed the people away from their current political and economic situations to focus on life after death and the salvation of their souls in heaven. In this way the Bible served to reinforce the oppression of the poor and to counter the people's hopes for more freedom and self-determination. Moreover, in recent times, Asian women have discovered the male bias in the Bible that calls for exposure and reinterpretation, if the Bible is truly to be Good News for all.

Asians have now begun to reclaim the Bible in a new way, rereading it through third-world eyes, through women's eyes. In this manner, the Bible, as the liberating word it was meant to be, can become a book of inspiration moving Asians to a spirituality that opens up new horizons of faith and hope in freedom and humanization, for both men and women alike.

The two approaches to Bible study included here typify the efforts of Asian theologians to rediscover a liberating spirituality by reading Scripture from a new perspective. Throughout the Bible study sessions, the participants were excited to discover ways in which the Bible could be read — from the standpoint of the victims of society, and to experience how the liberating and befriending Holy Spirit inspires us to read the Bible as God's word.

Carlos Abesamis from the Philippines compares how Jesus, "orthodox" Western Christians, and the poor and oppressed in the Third World would look at Mark 1:14–15. He first describes how he feels Jesus intended the text, and then he asks how we have been taught by the "Graeco-Roman, Western" missionary teachers. He encourages Asians to struggle with alternative interpretations of the text from their Asian perspective. Abesamis concludes that "the third look [that of the poor and oppressed] is very close to the first look [that of Jesus], in a way in which the second look is not." He concludes that since the Bible is the book of the poor and oppressed, the poor have the privilege of claiming their correctness in reading the Bible.

The second Bible study, prepared by Milburga Fernando of Sri Lanka and Marianne Katoppo of Indonesia, presents the text of Genesis 1:1–4:22 from a woman's perspective. They show how this text has been misused for the structure of domination, and how it has been "spiritualized" for the purpose of oppression. Rereading and reinterpreting the text from the perspective of the struggling poor and especially of women, a new image emerges, which is, according to Fernando and Katoppo, an image of "structures of communion." These structures of communion demonstrate the image of God as "mutuality, reciprocity, interdependence, complementarity, and partnership." For Fernando and Katoppo, liberation has to do with the restoration of the structures of communion through Christ in terms of "liberation and dignity in economic, political, social, religious, and spiritual terms."

Reading the Bible from a different perspective and through the eyes of the hitherto voiceless peoples is both daring and empowering. For us Asians, as we struggle together to understand and hear the word of God through Scripture in and through our collective experience of struggle, we can truly understand it as a source of liberation spirituality that will open to us God's will in human history.

A Third Look at Jesus and Salvation: A Bible Study on Mark 1:14–15

Carlos H. Abesamis

Introduction

Now after John was arrested, Jesus came to Galilee, proclaiming the good news of God, and saying, "The time is fulfilled, and the kingdom of God has come near; repent, and believe in the good news." (Mark 1:14–15)

This Bible study could bear several possible titles: "A Reflective Reading of Mark 1:14–15," "Basic Insights into the New Testament," or "A Third Look at Jesus and Salvation."

There is a need for a third look at Jesus and salvation. Worthwhile things are always worth a second look, but in the case of Jesus, we need a third look as well. The first look is the way Jesus looks at himself. The second look is the Graeco-Roman, Western look—the view most of us have grown up with during the last nineteen hundred years. It is time for a third look. This third look happens to be also the third-world look at Jesus. It is the view from the prism of the struggling poor. The third look is very close to the first look, in a way in which the second look is not.

A few examples are helpful at this point. For both the first look and the third look, "eternal salvation" is understood as "fullness of life," while for the second look it means the "life of the soul." This type of dichotomy between "soul" and "body" in the second look is also evident in its view of anthropology in which the soul (Greek *psyche*) is seen as a separate part joined to the body to constitute a human being. In both the first and third look, the human being is seen as a whole person (cf. Hebrew *nephesh*). In its original sense, the "greatest commandment" has an expansive meaning. It is translated in the first look as "love/justice/compassion/faithfulness" (cf. Matt. 23:23), and in the third look as "love/justice"; while in the second look, it is limited to "love."

It becomes evident that the third look has a closer affinity to the first. However, in order to understand the third look, we need to use an indispensable exegetical instrument, namely, the eyeglasses of the struggling poor of the Third World.

Mission of Jesus

What was the mission of Jesus? A second-look answer would be that Jesus was to die for our sins. The words from theology and catechesis that are associated with this view would be sin, spiritual grace, souls, heaven, seeing God face to face forever. The concomitant spirituality tends to be other-worldly, that is, concerned with souls, individualistic, moralistic, and so forth. How would we evaluate this "second look" at the mission of Jesus? It is indeed basically correct and biblical (cf. Rom. 5:6–10; 1 John 4:10; John 3:16; Matt. 1:21; Mark 10:45; 1 Cor. 15:3ff.), but it is inadequate.

The third look rediscovers the testimony of a key statement in Mark 1:14–15 and many similar testimonies in which the mission of Jesus is spoken of in terms of the proclamation of the "Kingdom of God." Now the "Kingdom of God" cannot be equated with the salvific death on the cross, for long before the cross, the "Kingdom of God" was "already in the midst of you" (Luke 17:21).

Thus we must find a formulation that is fair to the biblical data. This entails, among other things, a recognition that biblical texts are formulated from various points of view.

From the vantage point *on the cross,* or at some point before the cross, when Jesus became aware of his impending death and accepted it as an atoning death for sin, Jesus' mission was to die for sin. Thus possibly: "For even the Son of man came not to be ministered unto, but to minister, and to give his life as ransom for many" (Mark 10:45).

Taking a vantage point *after Jesus' resurrection* and looking back on Jesus' life, we can say that Jesus' mission was to die for sin. Thus: "And she shall bring forth a son, and thou shalt call his name Jesus: for he shall save his people from their sins" (Matt. 1:21).

From the vantage point of *eternity,* we can say that Jesus' mission was to die for sin. Thus: "Herein is love, not that we loved God, but that God loved us, and sent the Son to be the propitiation for our sins" (1 John 4:10).

But the vantage point from *inside history,* Jesus' mission was *originally* and *initially* to proclaim the Reign or Kingdom of God in word and action. Jesus' initial and original mission was the proclamation of final salvation in terms of the Reign or Kingdom of God (Mark 1:14–15; Matt. 11:2–6; Luke 6:20). Thus, "Now after John was arrested, Jesus came to Galilee, proclaiming the good news of God, and saying, 'The time is fulfilled, and the kingdom of God has come near; repent, and believe in the good news' "(Mark 1:14–15).

Reign or Kingdom of God

And what is the "Kingdom of God?"

The typical answers of the second look are "heaven," "the Church," "God's reign in our hearts." However, the third look evaluates the answers of the second look and says that these answers are at the least inadequate, if not altogether wrong. The third look bases its evaluation on the Bible itself.

From Isaiah

The third look takes the meaning from the vocabulary and symbols of the book of Isaiah (cf. Isa. 52:7; 40:9; 35:5–7; 29:18–21; 61:1–2; 58:6–7; 42:1–4; 25:8). As creatively reread by Jesus, the Reign or Kingdom of God is associated with:

- health to the sick
- life to the dead
- good news to the poor
- liberty to captives
- freedom to the oppressed
- final jubilee year of the Lord.

Thus, though the words "Reign" or "Kingdom of God" do not explicitly appear, Jesus was talking about them in the following central episodes:

The disciples of John told him of all these things. And John, calling to him two of his disciples, sent them to the Lord, saying "Are you he who is to come, or shall we look for another?" . . . And Jesus answered them, "Go and tell John what you have seen and heard: the blind receive their sight, the lame walk, lepers are cleansed, and the deaf hear, the dead are raised up, the poor have good news preached to them. And blessed is he who takes no offense at me." (Matt. 11:2–6; Luke 7:18–23)

And he came to Nazareth . . . and he went to the synagogue . . . And he stood up to read . . . the book of the

prophet Isaiah ... where it was written,
"The Spirit of the Lord is upon me,
because he has anointed me to preach good news to
the poor.
He has sent me to proclaim release to the captives
and recovering of sight to the blind,
to set at liberty those who are oppressed,
and to proclaim the acceptable year of the Lord."
And he closed the book ... And he began to say to them,
"Today this scripture has been fulfilled in your hearing."
(Luke 4:16–21)

From the Beatitudes

The meaning of the Reign or Kingdom of God can also be reconstructed from the beatitudes (Luke 6:20–21; Matt. 5:3–10). The second portion of the beatitudes are various names or aspects of biblical salvation. In other words, the Reign or Kingdom of God is a generic name for salvation. The second part of each beatitude represents specific aspects of salvation or the Reign or Kingdom of God. The beatitudes as reported by Luke read:

> Blessed are you poor,
>   for yours is the kingdom of God.
> Blessed are you that hunger now,
>   you shall be satisfied.
> Blessed are you that weep now,
>   you shall laugh. (Luke 6:20–21)

The beatitudes are reported by Matthew as:

> Blessed are the poor in spirit,
>   for theirs is the kingdom of heaven.
> Blessed are those who mourn,
>   for they shall be comforted.
> Blessed are the meek,
>   for they shall inherit the earth.
> Blessed are those who hunger and thirst
>   for righteousness,

for they shall be satisfied.
Blessed are the merciful,
    for they shall obtain mercy.
Blessed are the pure in heart,
    for they shall see God.
Blessed are the peacemakers,
    for they shall be called children of God.
(Matt. 5:3–9)

Taking the Lucan version of the poor and the hungry as the more original formulation, we reconstruct the following:

The Reign or Kingdom of God — based on the beatitudes — is a New World and a New History . . . where the poor and oppressed have been delivered from poverty and oppression, where those who mourned now rejoice, where there is no hunger, where the land now belongs to the humble, where people who have shown *hesed* will experience *hesed*, where people have a direct experience of God as "Father."

"Good News to the Poor"

One of the recurring themes in the key statements above is the seemingly innocent phrase "good news to the poor" or "blessedness to the poor." The second look has tended to neglect, ignore, or spiritualize this datum of the tradition.

Who Are the Poor?

The second look generally refers to the spiritually poor. The third look, however, is not content with a purely spiritualized meaning, for a more careful reading of the Bible reveals that the term "poor" refers to something very concrete and real. In the Book of Isaiah, which forms the inspiration and basis of Jesus' understanding, in all but possibly one instance, *anawim* always refers to the really, materially poor when it speaks of joy or good news to them (Isa. 3:15; 10:1–2; 11:4; 26:5–6, and so forth).

In the gospels, it is instructive to note that *ptochos* always refers to the really poor, except in the one isolated instance in

Matthew 5:3. In other words, whereas in the gospels "poor" always means the really poor except when qualified (and it is qualified only once, and not by Jesus but by Matthew), in the centuries-old post-biblical tradition, the second look has performed a great reversal; it has interpreted the "poor" of the gospels as "spiritually poor" and thus used one secondary verse, Matthew's 5:3, to interpret the others (Mark 14:5–7 and Matt. 26:9–11; Mark 10:21 and Matt. 19:21 and Luke 18:22; Luke 14:13; Luke 14:21; Luke 16:19–22; Luke 19:8; Luke 21:1–4 and Mark 12:42; John 12:5–8; John 13:29).

Whenever the gospels tackle the theme "good news to the poor" (also joy or blessedness to the poor), the writers always use "poor," with the single exception of Matthew. This would seem to indicate that the tradition is strong and uniform — the good news is to the really poor.

Therefore, although in Qumran, for instance, "poor" might refer to a non-materially-poor community, there is a strong indication that Jesus himself referred to the really poor.

What Is the Good News?

The second look has assigned a variation of the following as the gospel to the poor:
— Jesus is with you in your poverty. You can remain in your poverty.
— With Jesus you can bear it all.
— You are God's special favorites. You can bear your poverty with the strength and love he lavishes on you.
— Jesus will die for your sins on the cross.

The Sermon on the Mount

The third look says the obvious. It is the good news to the poor of any era — the good news of justice and their liberation from poverty and oppression! The gospel to the poor and oppressed must include this at the very least. Many other blessings, among them spiritual, constitute the gospel to the poor, but it cannot be gospel without justice and liberation.

How Central is the "Good News to the Poor?"

Look at the pivotal mission texts above:
— Matt. 11:2–5 = Luke 7:18–23

— Luke 4:16–21
— Luke 6:20 = Matt. 5:3

One or the other element in Jesus' mission may be omitted, but the one constant element mentioned in these central mission texts is "good news to the poor."

Structures of Communion and Structures of Domination: A Biblical Reflection on Genesis 1:1 to 4:22

Milburga Fernando and Marianne Katoppo

Introduction

The theologian's task is not to dominate the community by making decisions for others or by reflecting for others, but to provide the necessary biblical symbols so that people do their own reflections against the background of their own life experiences and in the wider text of life in the light of the Bible as brought out in these biblical symbols. Children and youth, and not only adults, are all quite capable of making their own reflections. If they are trained to reflect like this, very soon we will have a mature laity.

Our efforts at theologizing and interpreting the Bible from the point of view of the text of life that is our social reality will be sterile unless we include the vast masses of the people of our Asian countries.

We would like to bring out the situation of "security" of the masses of these people. Where do we place our security? Is it in God and God alone, or is it in a bank account, or in prestige, power, and wealth? Those who trust in God and not in power will interpret their life situations in the light of God's word more authentically.

The goal of theology is not knowledge. It is communion and fellowship and the restoration of right relationship among humankind. This communion and fellowship is also the distinguishing mark of theology that separates it from the other sciences.

Structures of Communion

God creates water and humans. Both these symbols mean life. Although water is sometimes understood as a life-destroying threat, as seen in the first chapter of Genesis it is considered a life-giving blessing. In the Israelite world in the ancient Near East, people knew what a blessing it was to have water and to have humans till the ground and produce food.

God creates freedom for humankind. With freedom human beings can choose certain things to eat and certain things not to eat. Animals have no freedom. Only people can choose freely. But their freedom is for what? Freedom to commit oneself to build structures of freedom, love, and communion.

God creates man and woman equally. In the first chapter of Genesis, nothing is said about the number, or the order, of human beings that were created. The late Christoph Barth, a professor of Hebrew, always said that here is a great manifesto of human equality. Verses 26 and 27 just tell us that God said, "Let us make the human person in our image and so God created the human person in God's own image, in the image of God, God created the human person, male and female, God created them" (translation ours). It is a very old fragment of poetry, far older than the rest of the Priestly manuscript in which it is embedded.

There is a second creation account in chapter 2 of Genesis. Whatever the differences between chapters 1 and 2, they both proclaim the equality of human persons. Of course, some might protest that man, being created first according to chapter 2, is superior to woman. To which one answer is, "Yes, and cats and dogs and koala bears were all created before man, so the day man takes orders from any of these animals, woman will accept the superiority of man!"

Or some might argue against equality because woman was created to be "helper." "Helper" in the Bible means the "help that comes from God" (Pss. 121:2; 146:5; 33:20; 44:26). "Helper" is never used in the sense of "servant" and does not express subordination or material help.

Or it might be argued that since the man "named" the woman Eve (Gen. 3:20), "naming" is construed as domination, or inferiority of the named to the namer. But "naming," especially for us in Asia, denotes or expresses relationships. What I name is related to me. In Indonesia, as in many parts of Asia, one rarely addresses another simply by name without adding some word denoting relationship: for example, *ibu* meaning "mother." And when the man names the woman in this creation story, he emphatically affirms her oneness, her equality with him. Notice how joyfully this is done:

> This at last is bone of my bones
> and flesh of my flesh,
> She shall be called Woman
> because she was taken out of Man.
> (Gen. 2:23)

The two humans are of one essence. We all know that in actual fact it is man who is born out of woman, but this verse is not to be read like a bank statement. Again, it is very ancient poetry with its roots deep in the primordial human experience, of man and woman belonging together, being of one substance, one essence.

And this is the bearer of God's image: mutuality, reciprocity, interdependence, complementarity, partnership. Not just woman-man, but all creation. All creation according to God's plan is based not only in gratuitousness but also in God's just government of the world—*mishpat*—as Gustavo Gutiérrez put it (see *On Job*).

God creates man and woman as one flesh. This means that all humanity has a strong bond of brotherhood/sisterhood and communion. In this relationship only a structure of love and communion is liberating. This structure of communion is compared to a globe. It cannot be compared to a circle that has just one center and the rest is periphery. Every point on the globe's surface is a center. This sense of communion is the meaning of John (1:14) when he says that Jesus pitched his tent among them—among human beings. He emptied himself and became one of the humans.

How do we prove that a structure is one of brotherhood/sisterhood of communion? What is the quality of such a structure? In the structure of communion and brotherhood, the first is the last and the last is the first. Everybody in it has the power to decide. Even in the Old Testament we often see the preference given to the younger. If there is a king, he is a servant king as in the servant psalms. The king is the person who washes the feet. We should be like Jesus and adopt the practice of making the last the first. This model structure of communion should find its place in baptism, marriage, and the eucharist. In all our institutions today there is so much domination and lording over the weak by the strong. Can we not, therefore, call all hierarchical structures sin?

"Just government," at present so far from being realized, is in fact God's plan for the world. This we reaffirm when we say "Our Father," meaning God is the source of life and love to all creation. Also, when we pray "Your will be done," God's will is the wholeness—the perfect joy of creation. "Holy be your Name"—how true is that when all over the world human persons, bearers of God's image and name, are being killed, tortured, oppressed? As Bartolomé de Las Casas said more than four hundred years ago, "the unjust death of millions before their time" is the problem we have to face.

Structures of Domination

Chapter 3 of Genesis uses two symbols, those of the serpent and of nakedness. The serpent is seen as the archenemy of the human being. This probably reflects a real experience of Palestinian agricultural society. Nakedness in the Bible means vulnerability, weakness, helplessness, or being open. Before the Fall the man and the woman were not disturbed though they were naked. After the Fall, when relationships were dislocated and disrupted, they became exposed to the violence of each other.

The sin envisaged is a certain act of disobedience—choice of domination instead of communion and interdependence. Knowing good and evil implies being like God. The "appetite" makes the man and the woman crave power, prestige, and wealth, the usual trappings of a king or queen.

The Idea of Kingship

The Mesopotamian king demanded allegiance from his subjects, and the people had to make offerings to the king. In Egypt too the king demanded respect from the people, and the people looked after the king. In Israel there was no king, for in Israel only God was king. "God is king" means no one dominates, no one exploits, and no one alienates another. Absolute obedience is given to God alone and to no one else. The term used is "God reigns." No one has special privileges, prestige, or power. The person given the title of "king of Israel" is a servant king who is meant to serve the subjects, that is, a leader always at the service of the people. No absolute obedience is given to earthly superiors or anyone except to God. Thus, the absolute obedience expected of woman is not to be given to man but to God.

In Exodus, having a king is connected with Baal worship. Why did God ask the Israelites not to worship other gods? The idea of freedom meant that one should not be dominated by anyone, not even by God. God never dominates, because "it is Yahweh who freed you." The God of Israel is not like Baal or Moloch who devours the sacrifices of the poor.

In Mark's Gospel, there is the phrase, "You are my beloved son in whom I am well pleased." "You are my beloved son"—meaning you are a king; "in whom I am well pleased"—meaning you are a servant, an idea taken from the Servant Songs (see Isaiah). And immediately after this what do we find? The temptations of Jesus. What are these temptations? How was Christ tempted? He was tempted to choose prestige, power, and wealth—the trappings of an earthly king.

In response to the question of Jesus to Peter, "Who do people say that I am?", the answer is given in Mark, "You are the Christ." It does not say "Son of God" because "Son of God" implies a king, and a king should automatically opt for prestige, power, and wealth. A person who dies on the cross cannot be a "Son of God" in that sense.

Structures of Domination in Society

In Genesis 4:17, we see Cain's generation building a town. Cain built a city and called it after his son's name, Enoch. There is always political domination in city building. City building creates a bridgehead to draw out the best of the resources from the city. In turn, masses of city people become alienated and dislocated to the margins, to the underside of the city, and to the countryside. This political power structure slowly causes death to the poor and impoverishes them even more.

Further, we read, "and Jubal Cain was the ancestor of all metal workers in bronze and iron." What do these things signify? That a murderer's son has built a city. That a murderer's son is responsible for technology. In this sense, there is blood in our culture today. There is blood in our history today. We find this structure of domination and the results of domination in culture, politics, and technology. The structure of communion has been broken and disrupted, and a hierarchical structure of domination has taken its place. This is all the consequence of listening to the "appetite."

Today, this structure of domination reaches an ugly climax in the recent Beijing massacre of the students clamoring for reforms:

> the beast, crazed
> turning upon its own children
> smashing them with its armoured tail
> the cries of freedom are smothered
> in the rivers of blood
> washing the square of heavenly peace
> and the children cry no more.
>   (M. Katoppo, June 4, 1989)

Conclusion

Liberation involves the restoration of fallen humanity through Christ. It is a liberation from sin, represented by the gods of power and possessions and by the milieu of violence, both personal and institutional. It is seen in terms of liberation and dig-

nity in economic, political, social, religious, and spiritual terms
(Ps. 144:12–15).

This liberation is a modeling on Jesus the servant-Lord. This
servant-lordship means humankind's dignity as the *chargé d'af-
faires* of God's creation, a dignity that is a responsibility for the
whole of creation—humanity and all. But this lordship comes
from communion and not from domination. The life of Jesus
illustrates the claim that victory and lordship of the cosmos come
not by domination but by humble and self-sacrificing service to
humankind and respect for creation. Since human beings were
created for communion and fellowship (*koinonia*), liberation
must be seen not only in individualistic terms, but definitely in
terms of the wider community together experiencing liberation
and dignity. This is the meaning of being accountable to one
another and to God.

Liberation, then, is a process and a pilgrimage. It starts off
with the experience of God through human beings and situations
(Exod. 34:29–35). This experience of God leads to repentance,
a turning away from the nasty face of human existence to the
example of Christ.

For us in Asia who live in a multireligious situation, respect
for this situation means an attitude of proexistence—a respect
for one another so that the best of each one will blossom into
its full flowering. This respect means having the sensitivity and
following the practice of the servant-Lord.

10

The Search for a Liberation Spirituality in Asia[1]

ATC III Participants

> In the beginning
> God made heaven and earth
> The earth was without form and void
> and the Spirit of God
> Brooded over the surface of the waters.
>   (Gen. 1:1-2)

Asia . . . .
We pause in silence
Before the awesome reality of Asia,
Her vastness, variety and complexity,
Her peoples, languages, cultures,
The richness of her history
And the present poverty of her peoples.

We take Asia to our hearts,
See her and feel her within us,
Embrace her
In her wholeness and brokenness,
While her rivers and tears flow through us,
Her winds, her sighs, her spirits,
Her moans, her howls blow within us.

There is a rich Asia
And a poor Asia;
Richness and poverty exist between nations
And inside nations.
But the stark reality stands out
Most of Asia is poor.

It is a continent of vibrant religiousness,
Of living faiths: Confucianism, Taoism,
Buddhism, Islam, Hinduism, Shamanism,
Christianity, and primal religions.

It is a continent of vast ethnic differences,
A diversity of cultures and indigenous traditions
Which enrich Asian countries.

Though rocked by division and conflicts
there is in Asia an emerging political consciousness.
People seek justice,
demand basic human rights,
struggle for freedom and self-determination
in their endeavor to promote life.

On arriving in Korea
a country divided for well nigh fifty years
and even before we begin our work
we are saddened to hear
that Christians working to overcome this division
are oppressed, detained, imprisoned.

In this challenging scenario
forty women and men
from different parts of Asia
converge at Suanbo in Korea.
Amidst the fragrance of pine, fir, and limestone hills
our spirits fuse.
Together we search
for a spirituality

that will free us
from all that shackles and dehumanizes.

In our search dawns
the realization that we are hemmed in
by obstacles on all sides:
socioeconomic, political, cultural,
religious, personal, and psychological.
Obstacles that stifle truth,
distort good,
mar beauty,
destroy unity and harmony,
deface humanity
and pervert creation.

Our religious institutions
are patriarchal and
overinstitutionalized.
They stunt human growth,
rendering us silent spectators
and accomplices
in situations of injustice.

We discern these realities.
We arrive at fresh insights
into sources of a spirituality
that is freeing all
from the principalities and powers
of this world.

We affirm the value of nonverbal,
nontextual, and nonscriptural
religiocultural sources
from which have irrupted into history
a variety of liberation movements:
the tribals, the *dalits*, the minjung,
the Cordillera people, the peasants,
human rights activists, women,
youth, peace and ecology groups.

An authentic spiritual strength emanates
from their liberating "primal visions"
and common life experiences.

We recognize creative spiritual resources
born of music, poetry, dance,
plays and dramas,
myths and legends,
folklore and cultural forms
connected with cosmic religiosity,
animistic cults,
and shamanistic practices
with their catalyzing forces,
constituting the total ethos of our people.

The source of our Asian liberation spirituality
is the Asian people's struggles against oppression,
the history of such struggles,
and hopes for a better future.
The memory of such struggles
and hopes is enshrined
in our people's sacred scriptures,
stories and celebrations.

The Christian Bible is in itself
the story of the Judaeo-Christian struggles
for liberation.

For us
these memories and scriptures are precious.
The memory of Jesus
is particularly important for us.
His life, death, and resurrection
are for all of us
summons and inspiration
to liberation praxis.

What, then, is spirituality?

Spirituality for us is bound up with life
and all that life involves.
It is freedom and food,
dignity and equality,
community and sharing of resources.
It is creativity and celebration
of the God of life and liberation.

Spirituality originates
from the Spirit of God
who fills the earth,
who gives, guides, and accompanies,
blesses, accepts, and works with.
Spirituality is
contemplation and praxis.
It is all that can contribute
to the balance and blossoming,
the healing and wholeness of life,
of the human race,
the earth,
the cosmos.

Spirituality contains two aspects:
OPENNESS and RESPONSE-ABILITY.
Openness to all humans,
all of nature,
from atoms and molecules
to the ultimate mystery we call God.
Response is the second moment,
a relevant reply to the need at hand,
the cry of the situation,
the call of God
that comes through people and events.

In the process of liberation
the reality of violence surfaces
sooner or later.
Asian peoples
are said to be tolerant,

passive, and fatalistic.
But down the centuries
Asian peoples have been known
to resist oppression fiercely.
The term "violence"
is used by oppressors
to hide their oppression
and denigrate any resistance
to their supremacy.

In the face of State oppression
and institutional violence,
armed resistance is sometimes unavoidable.
But we Christians are ill at ease
when arms are resorted to.
Violence breeds violence,
intensifies hatred and contempt,
and divides God's people.
We value the tradition
of respect for life.

The martyrs who have sacrificed
their lives for justice and life
are showing us that
the cross
remains the paradigm
of kenosis — self-emptying
in the Christian liberation struggle.
The cross
leads to resurrection
when it transforms the forces of oppression
and becomes redemptive.

Sexism,
a manifestation of patriarchy,
is sin.
The concept and reality of sexuality
are distorted.
But humanity needs to become aware

that our ancient cultures
view human sexuality in its wholeness.
Sexuality stands for beauty
and creativity of humans
as the image of God
and portrays mutual need
and interdependence.
As an authentic basis of common life
in community and communion,
it is part of human spirituality.

We condemn all attempts to distort
and pervert human sexuality,
in pornography, the film
and advertising media,
the commercialization of sex,
the abuse of the female body,
and its use as a commodity.

Patriarchal attitudes
degenerate the value system
and disintegrate the moral fiber.
They abet human eradication
through a process of human violence
whose victims are the poor,
the "diminutive" at the grass roots
amongst the formidable banyan trees
they are the marginalized,
and the majority are women.

Integral to our search
for a new spirituality
is a vision
of a new social order that is human and humane
demanding the restructuring of society
on an entirely new basis.

This vision calls
for a safeguarding of the diversity

and plurality of our peoples.
It demands the organization of society
where will blossom
economic, social, political,
and religious space for all.

Such a society can only emerge
through the empowerment
of the people at the periphery
— the oppressed and disinherited —
to determine their destinies,
live life to the full
in harmony with self,
others, and nature.

This vision is revolutionary.
It seeks to open prisons,
remove blinkers,
set free the downtrodden.

It speaks of a community
of women and men
equal and free,
the celebrants of an unfragmented
and wholesome earth
and the God of creation.

In unity, solidarity, and humanhood
we march ahead
to face the challenges
and stem the rot.

Our strategies include
reclaiming our history,
reinterpreting our scriptures,
redefining our images,
retelling our myths and proverbs,
legends, and stories —
insofar as they diminish us.

Reconciling ourselves to our ancestors,
we reappropriate our human dignity
through self-realization.

We are building links in a chain
that cannot be broken —
the chain of experience,
welded in love
and strengthened by commitment.

We do so through
our ABILITY to RESPOND,
our OPENNESS to REALITY,
our HARKENING to the SPIRIT —
the ultimate repository
of the power that propels us.

In conclusion
we believe with Kim Ji Ha

> Rice is heaven.
> As we cannot own heaven alone
> We should share rice with one another.
> As all share the light of the heavenly stars
> We should share rice and eat rice
>   together.

Notes

1. Subtitled "The EATWOT Experience," this final statement was originally written by Dalston Forbes (Sri Lanka), Bert Cacayan (Philippines), and Stella Faria (India).

Bibliography of Further Readings

Abraham, K. C. *Break Every Yoke*. Bangalore: Ecumenical Christian Centre, 1983.

Abraham, K. C. *Third World Theologies: Commonalities and Divergences*. Maryknoll, N.Y.: Orbis Books, 1990.

Amaladoss, Michael. *Making All Things New: Dialogue, Pluralism, and Evangelization in Asia*. Maryknoll, N.Y.: Orbis Books, 1990.

Amalorpavadass, D. S. *Indian Christian Spirituality*. Bangalore: National Biblical Catechetical and Liturgical Centre, 1982.

Arai, Tosh and Ariarajah, Wesley, editors. *Spirituality in Interfaith Dialogue*. Maryknoll, N.Y.: Orbis Books, 1990.

Ariarajah, S. Wesley. *The Bible and People of Other Faiths*. Maryknoll, N.Y.: Orbis Books, 1989.

Asian Religious Traditions and Chrsitianity. Manila: Faculty of Theology, University of Santo Tomas, 1983.

Balasuriya, Tissa. "Contemplative Commitment," *Quest*, No. 112. Colombo: Centre for Society and Religion, 1991.

Balasuriya, Tissa. "Liberation of the Holy Spirit," *Ecumenical Review*, Vol. 43, No. 2 (April 1991), pp. 200-205.

Balasuriya, Tissa. "Mary and Human Liberation," *Logos*, Vol. 29, Nos. 1 and 2 (1990). Colombo: Centre for Society and Religion, 1990.

Christian Conference of Asia. *Crossing Borders for Justice: International Conference on TNCs and the Labor Movement, October 1990, Seoul, Korea*. Hong Kong: Christian Conference of Asia, Urban Rural Mission, 1991.

Chung, Hyun Kyung. *Struggle To Be the Sun Again: Introducing Asian Women's Theology*. Maryknoll, N.Y.: Orbis Books, 1990.

Ellsberg, Robert, editor. *Gandhi on Christianity*. Maryknoll, N.Y.: Orbis Books, 1991.

Fabella, Virginia and Oduyoye, Mercy, editors. *With Passion and Compassion: Third World Women Doing Theology*. Maryknoll, N.Y.: Orbis Books, 1988.

Fabella, Virginia and Park, Lee Sun Ai, editors. *We Dare To Dream: Doing Theology as Asian Women*. Maryknoll, N.Y.: Orbis Books, 1990.

Habito, Ruben L. F. *Total Liberation: Zen Spirituality and the Social Dimension.* Maryknoll, N.Y.: Orbis Books, 1989.

Hensman, C. R. "Agenda for the Poor Claiming Their Inheritance," *Quest*, No. 109. Colombo: Centre for Society and Religion, 1990.

Katoppo, Marianne. *Compassionate and Free: An Asian Woman's Theology.* Maryknoll, N.Y.: Orbis Books, 1980.

Koyama, Kosuke. *Mount Fuji and Mount Sinai: A Critique of Idols.* Maryknoll, N.Y.: Orbis Books, 1984.

Koyama, Kosuke. *Fifty Meditations.* Maryknoll, N.Y.: Orbis Books, 1979.

Küng, Hans and Ching, Julia. *Christianity and Chinese Religions.* New York: Doubleday, 1989.

Labayen, Julio X. *To Be the Church of the Poor.* Manila: CFA Publications, 1985.

Lee, Peter K. H. "Christianized Hsin-Hsing Spirituality," *Ching Feng*, July 1984.

MacInnis, Donald E. *Religion in China Today: Policy and Practice.* Maryknoll, N.Y.: Orbis Books, 1989.

Neo, Julma and Laird, Elleen, editors. *Prophets for the Third Millennium.* Manila: Claretian Publications, 1990.

O'Brien, Niall. *Revolution from the Heart.* Maryknoll, N.Y.: Orbis Books, 1991.

Panikkar, Raimundo. *The Silence of God: The Answer of the Buddha.* Maryknoll, N.Y.: Orbis Books, 1989.

Pobee, John S. and von Wartenberg-Potter, Bärbel. *New Eyes for Reading: Biblical and Theological Reflections by Women from the Third World.* Oak Park, Ill.: Meyer Stone Books, 1987.

Raguin, Yves. *Attention to the Mystery.* Mahwah, N.J.: Paulist Press, 1979.

Samartha, S. J. *One Christ—Many Religions: Toward a Revised Christology.* Maryknoll, N.Y.: Orbis Books, 1991.

Song, C. S. *Theology from the Womb of Asia.* Maryknoll, N.Y.: Orbis Books, 1986.

Song, C. S. *Third-Eye Theology: Theology in Formation in Asian Settings.* Maryknoll, N.Y.: Orbis Books, 1991.

Sugirtharajah, R. S., editor. *Voices from the Margin: Interpreting the Bible in the Third World.* Maryknoll, N.Y.: Orbis Books, 1991.

Suh, David Kwang-sun. *The Korean Minjung in Christ.* Hong Kong: Christian Conference of Asia, 1991.

Takenaka, Masao. *The Bible Through Asian Eyes.* Auckland: Pace Publishing, 1991.

Takenaka, Masao. *God Is Rice.* Geneva: World Council of Churches, 1988.

"Towards a Liberating Spirituality," *Voices from the Third World*, Vol. XIII, No. 1 (June 1990). Colombo: Centre for Society and Religion.

Tsim, T. L., editor. *The Other Hong Kong Report 1990*. Hong Kong: Chinese University of Hong Kong Press, 1991.

Vandana, Sister. *Social Justice and Ashrams*. Bangalore: Asian Trading Corporation, 1982.

Vattakuzhy, E. *Indian Christian Sannyasa and Swami Abhishitkananda.* Bangalore: Theological Publications in India, 1981.

Wilson, H. S., editor. *Spirituality and Theological Education*. Bangalore, Board of Theological Education of the Senate of Serampore College, 1986.

Zachariah, Mathai, editor. *Ecology and Spirituality*. Nagpur: India Peace Centre, n.d.